BEING A TRAINEE SOLICITOR

HOW TO SURVIVE AND THRIVE

TOM PROVERBS-GARBETT

Published September 2025
ISBN 978-1-9174473-1-7

Text © Tom Proverbs-Garbett; Typography © Bath Publishing

All rights reserved. No part of this publication may be reproduced in any material form (including photocopying or storing it in any medium by electronic means and whether or not transiently or incidentally to some other use of this publication) without the written permission of the copyright holders except in accordance with the provisions of the Copyright, Designs and Patents Act 1988 or under the terms of a licence issued by the Copyright Licensing Agency (www.cla.co.uk). Applications for the copyright owner's written permission to reproduce any part of this publication should be addressed to the publisher.

Tom Proverbs-Garbett asserts his rights as set out in ss77 and 78 of the Copyright Designs and Patents Act 1988 to be identified as the author of this work wherever it is published commercially and whenever any adaptation of this work is published or produced including any sound recordings or films made of or based upon this work.

The information presented in this work is accurate and current as at 1 September 2025 to the best knowledge of the author. The author and the publisher, however, make no guarantee as to, and assume no responsibility for, the correctness or sufficiency of such information or recommendation. The contents of this book are not intended as legal advice and should not be treated as such.

Bath Publishing Limited
Registered Office: 27 Charmouth Road, Bath, BA1 3LJ
Tel: 01225 577810; Email: info@bathpublishing.co.uk;
Website: www.bathpublishing.com
Bath Publishing is a company registered in England: 5209173

EU RP (for authorities only)
eucomply OÜ
Pärnu mnt 139b-14, 11317 Tallinn, Estonia
Email: hello@eucompliancepartner.com; Tel: +3375690241

For my girls

(and junior lawyers past, present and future)

CONTENTS

ABOUT THE AUTHOR	ix
FOREWORD	xi
INTRODUCTION	1
1 | BECOMING A SOLICITOR	**5**
A book about you	5
But I'm not nervous…	6
Our avatar guide: Alex	7
A note on terminology	8
The impact of the Covid-19 pandemic and remote working	9
It's *your* career: know how *you* work	14
PART 1: WHAT TO EXPECT	
2 | WHAT DOES TRAINING LOOK LIKE?	**19**
Structure	19
A brief impression of training	21
Where do trainees fit? (Or, what is the hierarchy?)	25
Trainees: a vital part of the team	30
(Briefly) Law as a business	32
Being practical	37
Takeaways	38
3 | THE FIRST DAY	**39**
Early thoughts	39
Walking in	42
Illustrative timetable	43
What then?	46
Takeaways	47

4 | TRAINING WHEN TRAINING — 49
Professional requirements — 50
Internal training opportunities — 51
External training opportunities — 52
Responding to training — 53
Impact on your career — 55
Takeaways — 56

SEAT 1: COMMERCIAL LITIGATION — 57

PART 2: DOING THE WORK

5 | CHEERFUL WORKING — 73
Attitude — 74
Presentation — 77
Doing the work — 81
Passion, personality and proactivity — 87
Takeaways — 87

6 | MANAGING MISTAKES — 89
First principles — 90
Emails – Teams – Slack etc — 90
A call-back to proactivity — 92
You are learning… — 94
How not to treat people — 94
Stress…and coping — 96
Takeaways — 99

7 | MANAGING TIME — 101
Time recording — 101
Effective time management — 109
Handovers — 114
Appraisals — 116
Takeaways — 118

SEAT 2: PLANNING — 119

8 | SUPERVISION — 129
Role of the supervisor — 130
'Good' and 'bad' supervision — 132
The PAL System — 133
Application of PAL — 138
What are you able to control? — 139
Personality — 141
Takeaways — 142

9 | YOUR COHORT AND OTHER SUPPORT — 143
Personality (reprise) — 143
More about your cohort — 144
Non-fee earning colleagues — 146
Office gossip — 148
Credibility — 151
Takeaways — 152

10 | CLIENTS — 153
Your approach to clients: what do they want? — 154
Building relationships — 156
Emails and tone — 158
Takeaways — 159

11 | FIRM LIFE — 161
Getting involved — 161
What's out there? — 162
Fitting it all in: the power of groups — 168
Takeaways — 169

SEAT 3: CORPORATE — 171

PART 3: COMPLETION AND BEYOND

12 | QUALIFICATION — 183
Think about the present — 183
Process — 184
Interview preparation — 186
Staying in touch — 188
Takeaways — 189

13 | SECONDMENT — 191
Types of secondment — 191
Reasons to consider it — 192
Adventures in Scandinavia — 196
Further study — 202
Takeaways — 204

14 | THE FUTURE — 207
The SQE: its pros and cons — 207
Generative AI — 210
Ethics — 213
Hybrid working — 214
Takeaways — 216

SEAT 4: SECONDMENT — 217

15 | FINAL THOUGHTS — 225

GLOSSARY — 229

DOUBLE DUTCH: A GUIDE TO JARGON — 239

ACKNOWLEDGMENTS — 243

INDEX — 245

ABOUT THE AUTHOR

Tom Proverbs-Garbett is a solicitor of 20 years' experience, during which time he's worked with many trainees and supervisors along with being both a trainee and a supervisor himself. A true believer in life-long learning, Tom is deeply invested in helping juniors to develop their professional as well as legal skills. Tom has postgraduate degrees in law, education, business, literature and creative writing, the combination of which produced this book. He is a fellow of the Chartered Governance Institute, the Institute of Corporate Social Responsibility, the Chartered Management Institute and the Royal Society of Arts. Tom is an in-demand speaker, trainer and consultant. He lives in the Midlands with his wife and daughters, surrounded by (his) Lego. Published widely, his debut collection of poetry – *The Adept* – was released in 2025.

FOREWORD

This book came 35 years too late for me – I wish Tom had been around during my trainee years to write it! It's a must-read for anyone considering or embarking on a legal career, full of practical advice and guidance which demystifies the exciting but daunting step into life as a trainee solicitor.

Reading *Being a Trainee...* made me reflect on my own career. It wasn't the most structured of starts.

I went to university through clearing after disappointing A-Level results and applied for a training contract a year after my friends at law school while I thought about the type of legal career that might interest me. That thinking time must have helped because once I'd found the firm for me, I stayed put. I'm now the Senior Partner of Pinsent Masons, the firm I joined as a trainee, so it all worked out in the end!

I found my way there using the tools set out in this book – working collaboratively, with passion, and taking ownership of my career. But without a roadmap I had to do this the hard way, learning as I went. In collecting so much experience and so many tips together in one place, Tom has created a wonderful resource to help the next generation along. Having this on my desk back in the day would truly have made a difference to my trainee experience.

It's fair to say the firm I now lead is very different to the firm I joined – it's way bigger, with broader capabilities and a global client base. And the experience of work is very different too. Yet, as Tom highlights, despite those differences in the firm (and between firms and areas of law) the underlying elements of the career of a solicitor remain the same: a rewarding mix of technical detail, people skills and common sense.

In many respects, that is the beauty of the legal sector – it changes and adapts while retaining its relationship with the past. The sector has been good to me and this book helps to explain why.

Andrew Masraf
Senior Partner of Pinsent Masons LLP
August 2025

INTRODUCTION

I'm sitting in a pub at eight in the morning somewhere near Old Street, on the edge of East London. The barman, still opening the shutters and welcoming a couple of keen regulars, eyes me suspiciously but gives me a coffee. On the house. I am terrified and must look it. Five years of studying, three interviews, tens of thousands in fees, and a healthy dose of self-doubt has got me to this point: it's the first day of my training contract.

As I sip the coffee and try to calm my nerves – I remember this quite clearly – I'm suddenly aware that walking into the imposing building on the edge of the City will be one of the most daunting things I will ever do. As it turned out, even leaving people to their cider on that first morning was a challenge, locked doors the manager's subtle indication that the pub didn't (officially) open until ten.

Why so daunting? The pressure, the sense of expectation was huge, but anticipated. The bit I hadn't readied myself for – *couldn't* – was the unknown: what the hell would the next two years be like? Sure, work experience (a vacation scheme, as it's known) gives some idea of the type of work involved at a commercial law firm – and how many people in the office enjoy a karaoke night out – but on that morning, in that pub, I realised that the immediate future was a blur.

I took each day as it came, survived, and enjoyed it. I found work I liked and qualified. I wouldn't say that I had a clear idea of what training would entail: I dealt with the challenges as they came. Fast forward eight years…

This book was born one run-of-the-mill Monday morning. A trainee in my team – first seat, perhaps two months into life as a lawyer, and of whom I was fond – handed me a piece of work. It was research I'd asked him to look at on the preceding Friday. Immediate alarm bells: he'd either bashed it out on Friday afternoon, desperate to get out to the pale sun (in which case it probably didn't have the detail I needed) or he'd locked himself away and worked on it over the weekend (something there was no need for – it wasn't urgent and I'd given him until the middle of the following week).

I took a look at what he'd produced. He'd broadly found the right answer (at least, it looked sensible and dealt with the right issue), but the note he'd provided was a 'cut and paste' job from various legal websites. He hadn't even changed the fonts.

Ok, it was only two months in, but I knew something about this guy – CVs tend to circulate in advance of new joiners. He'd done well at university; he'd organised and led various teams; he'd read for a masters; he'd made his way through a testing interview with two of the more terrifying partners at my firm. He'd elbowed his way into a career he really wanted. I was puzzled – where did this lack of effort come from?

We went for coffee.

'I just wondered how long you spent on it?' I asked.

'Well, most of Friday afternoon. I wanted to make sure you had it as quickly as possible.' A note of defensiveness. He could clearly sense that this wasn't a meeting to deliver praise. But the idea wasn't to make him feel bad – I genuinely wanted to know where the work had come from.

'I appreciate you prioritising it,' I chose my words carefully, 'but I did say I didn't need it until later in the week. And I was hoping for something that could go to the client, like we discussed. I mean, it seems to be lifted completely from [and here you can insert the name of your chosen legal research website]. You haven't even standardised the fonts, let alone put it in the firm's house style. It doesn't have a structure or further analysis: we're legal experts and wordsmiths; we don't just click and drop!' I paused and considered. 'I wanted, for want of a better word, some elegance.'

Delivering constructive feedback – as it's rather euphemistically called – is never pleasant, but we were talking about the basics. He looked mortified. My heart sank.

INTRODUCTION

'I just wanted to find the answer. I didn't think about anything else. I suppose I panicked; I was relieved I could find something to say!

I mean there's nothing to tell you how to put these things together. At law school we had examples of every form you could ever want to fill in, but working with people and working out how it's done in practice is…it's a learning curve, right? I guess I'm trying to find out what different people like, how they want the work done, and to put those messages together.'

I paused and, unexpectedly, realised he had a point.

To those who have been in practice for some time, it's second nature that the look of a document is important: presenting something neatly and logically implies command of your subject before anyone gets to the substance. But no-one tells you that; it comes with experience. Training is a challenge and a period of transition as you become a professional lawyer. You've been taught the basic skills during your academic and professional studies. What you don't have are instructions for approaching the professional legal world. In other words, a guide to your period of training.

I subsequently spoke to many trainees while thinking about this book and during its writing, reinforcing that view.

There was consensus that useful technical skills, started at law school, progressed pretty well during training. The academic side is prescribed: covered in the qualifying law degree, the Graduate Diploma in Law or alternative activity (the Chartered Institute of Legal Executives route or, more recently, apprenticeships).

What those trainees couldn't point to, at least in advance of turning up on their first day, was information about the training period itself. Yes, firms are fairly good at describing the work they do and the sectors they specialise in, major firms are generous with their vacation schemes, and many firms stand financially behind their preferred groundwork for practice (such as the legacy Legal Practice Course or the Solicitors Qualifying Exam (SQE) preparation courses). Yet there is little to no up-front discussion about how on-the-job training – such an important part of the route to qualifying as a lawyer in the UK – will pan out.

This book is intended to go some way to filling that gap. It's an extended chat over coffee, the kind you might have with a supervisor or a trainee just ahead of you when inevitably asking: 'How did you do it?'

As an introduction to professional practice, bespoke for lawyers, much of the content consists of common sense suggestions for improving your experience of training: how you might present yourself and your work in the most professional light. That doesn't undermine its importance. The advice may be obvious once explained – the best ideas are – yet if it was a given from the beginning, every trainee would feel prepared to succeed from day one and, as we know, that's not the case. Over time and by trial and error you are likely to discover this information for yourself; the good news is that by reading this book you can hot-wire the process.

I have been necessarily general. The idea is to give you a taste of what working in a law firm, as a lawyer, is like. I want to prompt you to think about how you will approach relationships with (and within) the teams you join, the work you might do, the social and volunteer activities you might get involved with and, of course, interactions with clients. These will be the major tasks for the initial stages of your professional life. Like an athlete visualising the upcoming race, imagining yourself in these situations before they arise – with the benefit of the context I'll give you – will put you at a huge advantage.

At the end of the book, I hope you will feel prepared for the issues that most trainees face and, rather than spending the first six months wondering what's expected of you, you can hit the ground running, wringing every drop of value from your training. To continue our athletics analogy: the race remains, but you will have a deep understanding of the challenges you may face on the track.

Oh, and that first-seat trainee I mentioned? He qualified into my department and more eloquent legal memos you'd be hard-pressed to find. You can do this. You will do this. I trust this book eases your path.

1 | BECOMING A SOLICITOR

As you are reading this, it's likely that you hope to train as a solicitor (or are currently doing so). After reading this book I want you to feel more connected with and secure about the career you have chosen and better informed about the two-year on-the-job training generally required for qualification. This is an honest look at how you might prepare for and make the most of those two years.

A book about you
This is a book about you. It's a self-help book in the pure sense: it won't pose or answer revelatory questions and it's unlikely to wholly change your life. That said, by reading it you will understand how to make life much, much easier for yourself – and how to stand out from the crowd – in the early stages of your legal career.

Put another way, the advice set out in this book is intended to allow you to create an individual bridge from the student you are to the lawyer you want to be. Indeed, the major point of evolution throughout your time as a trainee is developing the ability to curate both your approach to doing the work and your professional image, taking responsibility for *your* career and directing it wherever you want it to go.

'Curating' takes place through developing relationships within the firms and teams in which you work, answering the question: who are *you* as a lawyer? The advice in the following pages is designed to progress this idea of career ownership.

This book isn't an academic text, a practitioner's guide or a 'how to' toolkit. It doesn't set out a five-step plan guaranteed to impress your supervisor or bring you 'trainee of the year' at any awards dinner you care to attend. I wish I could write that book for you; I can't. There's no such thing as the perfect trainee, any more than the perfect lawyer. Every one of you will bring different skills to bear on your training. Each of you will need to deal with different personalities, to reconcile the ways of working of others with your own style, to learn and, most importantly, to recognise an opportunity for learning. Each of you will take a separate road: the firms you train at will be unique in terms of their work, character, and culture.

And yet those individual paths have commonalities – difficulties you will all face, albeit balanced by the highs of work done well and colleagues-made-friends. How you might ameliorate the difficulties and extend the positives is the subject of this book. What I hope to give you is advance notice of those areas where, in my experience, trainee lawyers tend to miss a trick. Why? Because they haven't envisaged themselves in the role. They – you – haven't thought through how you might act and react in specific professional situations. And how could you, without a guide?

'Isn't this all a bit negative?' a friend of mine said – a reader of an early draft and a partner at a top 20 firm herself. 'Aren't you going to paralyse them with fear?'

Ten minutes later – why is it that a contemporaneous come-back is always just out of reach? – I had two thoughts: (1) how flattering it is she thought circulation of more than ten copies was a possibility (see, we all have doubts); and (2) that it's not about fear at all. It's about preparation: what will a trainee life *actually* be like?

Having a sense of what the future could hold – in the broadest sense (there's no crystal ball) – will make the whole process less daunting. Or, for the benefit of my friend's scepticism, it will make the whole process *more exciting*, more immediately available to you. You don't have to wait and see how things pan out – you can begin to experience legal life right now.

But I'm not nervous...

Now, it may be that (so far) it hasn't occurred to you to be concerned or nervous about your legal journey, and, if so, I applaud that confidence. I really do. Nevertheless, this book is still for you.

Even the most robust character – and incidentally I think a moderate dose of worry will make you a better lawyer in the long run, but more of that later – will face moments of doubt. Perhaps there's been a misunderstanding about what has been asked of you. Perhaps there's concern about your performance of a task. Perhaps you're questioning the whole career after the third horrendously late night in a row. These are doubts everyone has at the beginning of their journey and, as we will discover, are almost entirely without foundation. Preparation, as the saying goes, is key.

Over the course of this book I will take the long view, sharing stories, best practice suggestions and tips for approaching your voyage from fresh-faced hopeful to qualified solicitor. Together we will explore why moving into the world of legal work can lead to trepidation, but we will banish that thought by considering the key stakeholders and potential allies to approach when we get stuck. In conjunction, we will identify strategies for dealing with uncertainties or (in the very worst case) conflicts that arise.

Along the way, we'll touch on 'how not to do it', likely to be the most valuable reason for reading this book. The worst mistakes have already been made, as one look at the legal press will show you. Some of these stories are no doubt apocryphal, but they are frequently both amusing and the source of good lessons. And a dose of humour will take you a long way in law, where the risk of self-importance is ever-present.

Our avatar guide: Alex

In an attempt to bring the training experience to life, we will follow our every-person trainee, Alex, through her two years of training. Alex is at a mid-ranking commercial firm, something I know won't reflect the experience of every one of you – what could? – but which gives scope for us to see how she handles interactions with a range of people: training supervisors, clients, peers. A situation where her experiences should be transferable.

It might seem a little indulgent to have a fictional character carving her way through a book such as this. And maybe it is. Yet it's much more than a bit of light relief. As I have already mentioned, helping you imagine how you might approach training is a central pillar of this book – there are few definitive rights and wrongs but lots of situations where it is useful to consider your position in advance. How would you react to an uncooperative supervisor? What opportunities for involvement in the life of the firm have your name written all over them? Seeing how Alex deals with some of these issues assists you, I hope, in envisioning your future.

Some of you may have had careers before becoming (or thinking of becoming) lawyers – I salute you. Others of you may have clear and individual ideas about how you intend to approach your training. I trust you still find something useful here: legal practice is a stimulating and fulfilling career, but it has certain idiosyncrasies that the following pages will examine. If nothing else, Alex's experiences will give you an idea of the trials and tribulations of the typical trainee. And any advice from those who have gone before you cannot be a bad thing. If it speaks to you, soak it up; if not, you have nevertheless received the benefit of experience beyond your own.

A note on terminology

We approach this subject at an interesting time. The very concept of the training contract is in a period of flux.

At the time of writing, would-be solicitors who by 2021 (broadly) hadn't started a law degree – presumably most, if not all of you – are only able to qualify by passing the SQE and undertaking a period of qualifying work experience. The previous qualification route, the Legal Practice Course and its accompanying two-year period of training which firms offered in one go as 'training contracts', is maintained by way of transitional arrangement only.

In practice, this has turned out to be largely semantics. In using the term 'a recognised period of work experience', the Solicitors Regulation Authority (SRA) has maintained the duration of training at two years but now permits it to be disaggregated – carried out in chunks. Most firms continue to refer to 'training contracts' in their recruitment materials and internal practices. The main result of the change is really the SRA's move

1 | BECOMING A SOLICITOR

away from managing and policing the training process directly.

Against that background, I have occasionally retained a reference to the 'training contract' in this book. In most cases, firms will still provide a two-year fixed term contract for trainees, and the terminology shows no sign of disappearing (at least in the near future). Still, nothing is static, and we will discuss in Chapter 14 the implications of the SQE and the future of training.

The practical advice in this book is designed to be of use to you regardless of the make-up of your training. Were the concept of traineeship abandoned altogether (and there is no suggestion of that at the time of writing), your first two years at a firm is likely to be structured similarly to the current training contract: it works and is deeply embedded in the psyche of firms and their lawyers. So, whether we discuss a training contract, a period of work experience or simply the early years of your professional life, the advice stands.

The impact of the Covid-19 pandemic and remote working

In 2020, we experienced an unprecedented and – whatever the powers that be try to tell us – irreversible change to the way we work. The Covid-19 pandemic made the unimaginable real, the unthinkable the norm. I guarantee that partners at whichever law firm you are thinking of joining would have said, if asked before the instruction to stay indoors, that working from home was for a select few part-timers at most. Certainly not the way to build a career. How times have changed.

It may not occur to you that there is any other way of working than a a hybrid model where work is split between home and the office. Yet this is a situation that has only come to fruition as a result of a monumental crisis. As is so often the way, need breeds change. If there is no choice but to work from home, home can be made to work.

There's growing divergence between those who think remote working is the new normal, providing the flexibility so many crave, and those that think not being in the office means the loss of something fundamental, ineffable: the spark which comes from being together, bouncing ideas off each other like free electrons to create something greater than the sum of our parts.

There is no doubt that working from home in some form gives an opportunity for balance – whether that's increased personal well-being in avoiding the draining monotony of a commute, satisfaction in being able to curate tasks outside work to your timetable rather than someone else's or simply working at a time that suits you and which aligns with your body clock.

While this change in the way we work has affected all businesses, it has had a particular impact in law. Despite what many law firms will tell you about their interest in innovation and their dramatically different strategies, they are by nature conservative. This is exactly as one might expect; they are, after all, established to manage legal risk. The role of precedent – what has gone before – is so deeply engrained that it forms the basis of day-to-day work. Change of any kind is not easy and often hard won. The pandemic forced law firms to act quickly and decisively, and you are now unlikely to find a firm that doesn't – at least in its marketing rhetoric – embrace some element of home working.

However, firms have struggled with how to make sure that new comers to the profession (you) stay engaged and enthusiastic if everyone is working from remotely at least some of the time. How do lawyers responsible for your training make sure you have the opportunity to pick up all those unteachable, sub-textual elements that can't be described or experienced from a distance?

Even in the 'not so old' days, and we're only talking 10 or 15 years ago, senior members of the profession would have their trainee sitting in their office in a corner desk away from the window. In many large and prestigious firms this remains the case. Yes, this sounds Dickensian and the very fact of sitting in someone's office at a corner desk marks you out as the junior in the room, but it had (and has) certain advantages. The partner/senior associate sitting by the window, your supervisor, can call over and ask you to amend a document, join a call, or just pull your chair up for a chat about life, the universe and everything (assuming you have a good

1 | BECOMING A SOLICITOR

supervisor – and more of that in Chapter 3). The situation is inherently conducive to learning – you pick things up by osmosis.

This is an extremely hierarchical model which means you (as a trainee) tend to be the preserve of your supervisor and, occasionally, others who report to them. But, again, there are advantages to such an approach. You work closely with your supervisor, get involved in all their work, leading to the invaluable experience of seeing projects through from start to finish (time permitting).

You also gain a broad overview of the behaviour of other members of the team, learning what it is like to be a senior lawyer. Never underestimate the experience gained from simply sitting in a room with someone and hearing how they approach telephone calls, colleagues, how they prioritise their work. It is their attitude and mannerisms as much as the content that you're soaking up.

You might have noticed, as perceptive and detail-orientated readers, that I started this section by saying this was commonly the case *a decade or so ago*. As you enter the profession today, you're unlikely to come across offices for individuals. There are notable exceptions but, in general, law firms like other professional services organisations have moved to an open plan arrangement. This mirrors the general working trend across the UK, the idea being that people cut off in offices aren't providing or experiencing (as the case may be) those learning experiences that we've just discussed. Open plan working also brings down the cost of real estate because you can fit more people into the same footprint and utilise the space in different ways.

Now the model has changed so that (in theory and, again, generalising hugely) it's more egalitarian. You're no longer the trainee stuck in the corner and your scope for learning has potentially increased: now you can listen to the interactions of those around you – your peers, those slightly more senior and those much more senior than you, both in your team and in other disciplines. To the extent your firm encourages 'hot-desking' – shorthand for having no fixed pattern for where you sit to work – you grab a desk wherever you feel comfortable (or, more likely, attempt to book through an impenetrable online system). Once in situ, you will be able to engage with different colleagues every day, inevitably exchanging views and broadening your horizons. As forensic science tells us, every contact leaves a trace.

Of course, human nature being what it is, hot-desking frequently means sitting at the same desk every day without being able to call it 'your' desk or leave anything on it.

That is one for the organisational psychologists to figure out.

The downside of this brave new world is that you're unlikely to be so involved with your supervisor; they may be sitting in an entirely different location, so you won't be able to pop over to ask a question. By function of the new geography, you become an 'asset' for the whole team. So, rather than being involved from start to finish in your supervisor's work, you might be involved more superficially in lots of projects for different members of the team at all levels of seniority. This can bring its own advantages because you get to see a whole swathe of additional transactions or other pieces of work you might not otherwise experience.

And so the wheel turns. There are pros and cons to all of this and (a cliché but it's true) there is no one-size-fits-all. If we add into the mix the legacy of the pandemic and the fact that people may not be in the office as much or at all, hopefully you can see the quandary facing those at the management end of law firms.

In good news, the work/life balance in law tends to have improved dramatically, with the use of virtual meetings vastly reducing the amount of travelling even if the hours remain long. Meetings in person may still be required to further a client relationship or to run a seminar effectively, but this is now the exception rather than the rule. You won't face – at least, not every day – the drudgery of a commute. Life is likely to be much more convenient for you. Yet what's missing is the passive learning you do simply by being in the office, being with other people and hearing about what they're working on, appreciating their way of approaching a problem, or seeing how they speak to clients, colleagues and other lawyers.

This is something that law firms are wrestling with. At the time of writing, some organisations require their people to be in the office four or five days a week. Others are making a virtue of hybrid, or even majority remote working, trying at the same time to find new ways to ensure that trainees (indeed all staff) remain engaged with the business of the firm and one another.

This has led to change. A common emerging practice includes mandating regular virtual check-ins between supervisor and trainee, meaning that relationship has maintained its importance. Specific remote working policies for trainees have also been launched which transcend department approaches – although teams commonly retain a wide level of discretion even under such policies. Most people simply ask trainees to be sensible and align with the practices of the rest of the team. This involves practical things like making clear where you are at any given time in your calendar, which other team members can access. It's not intended to be onerous.

The use of legal project managers is also becoming more prevalent. At first glance, that might be seen as solely a client benefit: a specialist project manager will be ideal for mapping out and keeping on track large commercial transactions or complex litigation. However, they're also really useful in making sure that people in an internal project team talk to each other – whether that's a daily five-minute meeting (a 'stand up') or a weekly half an hour – providing a safe forum for asking questions, giving comfort and support to those new to the business or new to their role. Given the semi-public setting, I encourage you to make sure that questions you ask don't have obvious answers (in the sense of being easily able to find them yourself should you have taken the time to look), but don't be afraid to speak up. Asking questions is critical for learning.

Some firms have taken the opportunity to reassess what they want from their trainees, who are, after all, the future of the business. Some have maintained the training contract format adding bespoke, specialist-directed training for a particular role rather than the general training of the past. This might, for example, be a training contract designed to produce from its alumni specialists in legal technology, or with focus on a specific area of law and its idiosyncracies rather than the more general training in distinctly separate areas of law that is typically offered. As departures from the norm, these innovations should, if working as intended, place the emphasis on outcomes from that unique training experience. This may reduce reliance on the passive osmosis of skills anticipated from being in the office.

Elsewhere, there remains the issue of bringing people together at some regular interval. However comfortable you think you might be working from home – and I have done so very happily for many years – it is important you get a sense of the professional community of which you are a part. This might manifest in any number of ways: the feeling of being in an office environment; hearing about professional developments; having lunch with colleagues; getting involved with social events. Each of these things is important and they have their own chapters in this book. As mentioned already, the approach taken by many firms to a solution is to devolve the decision to internal teams, allowing them to agree which day(s) they will meet. The problem that persists is senior people, from whom you will be so eager to learn, are those most likely to feel able not to attend.

It's your career: know how you work

This provides, I hope, a sense of what you will need to navigate as you join the profession. As with the rest of this book, the advice is to start to imagine how you might react to different opportunities, instructions or requests in context.

What do I mean by that?

Well, to give a simple example – and as we will discuss in much greater detail in Chapter 8, on negotiating the relationship with your supervisor – how might you approach asking questions? If you're sitting next to your supervisor, you might shout out questions as they occur (depending on the relationship you have). If you're working remotely, you might need a different plan, putting a meeting in their diary, say, for a virtual call. You won't be able to read body language in the same way. Perhaps you will be dealing with background noise if you or they are in the office. What steps must you take to make sure you get the input you need to carry out your role?

That's at a micro level. It's also worth thinking about what's important to you more broadly. At the outset of your career, you may not know quite how you prefer to work, the professional environment being sufficiently different from university or previous jobs to mean you need to reset your preferences – collaborative work is required, for example. Yet, if you are given a choice, think about what work looks like to you. Do you want to go into the office more frequently than those days a week when the team mandates a meeting? Firms are very conscious, as I've said, about the potential loss of collaboration. While I'm not convinced this is true (more on that below), you will want to learn as much as you can at this formative stage of your career. Remote working is likely to mean that you need to take charge of your own learning and development much earlier in your professional life.

By the time you're reading this, you'll understand the importance of self-directed learning and staying up-to-date with legal developments. When you join a firm, you will have all sorts of subject-specific online resources subscribed for by your firms. Without fail, these resources will have some sort of dedicated daily updates to which you can subscribe depending on your field of interest. Think about what you need to know, subscribe to those areas, and make the time to read them.

If you're at a firm with more limited resources, meaning you don't have access to those large databases, you can make use of RSS aggregators or even a simple Google notification setup works equally well. The outputs will be less targeted, but it enables you to keep up-to-date with specified developments. Identify the topics you want to know about and, even if 80% of the daily alerts aren't relevant, you're very unlikely to miss a major development and you can raise anything interesting with your supervisor or your fellow trainees.

Creating those relationships is even more important in the world of hybrid working. Regular catch-ups with your fellow trainees are perhaps the most helpful in figuring out, collectively, how you might approach the workplace. What are they struggling with? What hacks have they found? How frequently are they going into the office? Is it worth creating a regular lunch date to compare notes? (Of course it is.)

Right, so we have acknowledged the world of work has changed permanently and significantly. Yet it's not the work that has changed but, in my view, the newfound agency you have to engage with it. Any potential loss in opportunity for collaboration is a red herring. Five or even six days in the office every week meant familiarity, which as we all know breeds contempt. People were just trying their best to get through the day and whether the office was a Petri dish of fermenting ideas is moot. In the new world, people head into the office once, twice or three times a week where they tend to be more energised and looking for discussion and engagement. You can leave your flat looking forward to brainstorming with a colleague or meeting a client for a coffee; the detailed legal work as you draft those technical board minutes is probably much better done behind a closed door wherever you feel most comfortable.

To save repeating myself in the rest of this book, I won't keep referring to the pandemic. Its impact has sent shock waves through the working world and, as a result, you are likely to have choices that generations before you didn't. That's good news but requires thought and careful handling, from the firm and from you. For now, let's turn our attention to what you can expect from the practicalities of training, from your first day and onwards to the horizon of qualification.

PART 1: WHAT TO EXPECT

2 | WHAT DOES TRAINING LOOK LIKE?

We could start our investigation of training – and where maintained the training contract – from many jumping-off points. We could think about the work, or the people, or the challenge. All of these have substance; they are the meat and potatoes of the role. Yet this chapter is devoted to form and process. Why? Well, starting here gives us an overview of the structure of training in the context of a law firm's function and aims. From this perspective, we gain a general impression of the whole experience into which we can delve more deeply later on. After all, if you know nothing about training other than it's the way into a legal career (and for some of you, that's where you are), then addressing, 'What is it?' must be the starting point.

Let's begin by answering some scene-setting questions posed by a hypothetical incomer, such as: Where do trainees fit in to the law firm hierarchy? What is the business of law we intend to join? Once we have answers to these questions, we can move on to look at specific activities within this general framework.

By the end of the chapter, I want you to have a high-level overview of a typical training experience from start to finish, an understanding of the various roles in a law firm and their interaction, and some sense of the business world in which the law firm operates. Armed with this background, we can then start to look at where your energies are best spent as you enter the world of legal work.

Structure

I'd like to start by pointing you in the direction of some useful and often updated material provided by the regulator. The SRA regularly updates its Student Information pages on its website. While we won't consider this material in detail in this book, it sets out accessibly and comprehensively the mechanisms for qualification.

Our goal, however, is not to review the regulator's requirements (although they are, of course, very important) but rather to try to immerse ourselves in the experience of training in advance of joining a firm. It will do no harm at all to review what the SRA demands of you; for now let's concentrate on what you can expect from the training process.

In a typical case, the training contract (still the most regular approach to training) consists of four seats of six months each. Occasionally, one or two of those six-month blocks may be divided in two or some other configuration is used, such as six seats of four months. The structure will depend on the training format chosen by a particular firm; generally, however, the 4 x 6 model is most common.

This means that you will be able to explore four areas of legal practice. It doesn't sound very much, and it isn't, but the intention is to strike a balance between (a) exposing would-be lawyers to different areas of legal practice and to provide an overview of how a given team fits in to the work of the rest of the firm; and (b) making that experience meaningful. Too many moves will result in only superficial experience; too long in one seat and you lose opportunities for experience elsewhere. Three months is generally accepted as sufficient for trainees to achieve a high-level, working knowledge of an area, sufficient to make a helpful junior contribution, and for you to determine whether it would be interesting to commit to in the long term.

Most firms will have well defined and deeply embedded trainee schemes – departments and supervisors will be well versed in trainees arriving with them every six months or so. Supervisors will be accustomed to their role and the human resources team will have a system in place to allocate seats. The only real question for you, once you join, will be which areas of law you want to experience. At most firms, although not all, you will be asked to indicate preferences when you join and then as you go through the training process.

Making choices is difficult. Especially when it can feel like the decision will have major consequences for your future. Most people in your situation spend time trying to rationalise matters, to reason to a solution, but your preferences can just as easily be dictated by a general feeling.

So, you might think that you enjoyed land law at university (someone has to) and so definitely want to spend time in the property team. You might have shadowed a barrister specialising in family law and want to spend time in the family and probate team. You might have watched *Suits* and decided that litigation is where you truly belong. None of this, even the last, is wrong. There *is* no 'right'. Anything that draws you towards a particular area is perfectly acceptable – try it and see what you like and what you don't.

In fact, the decision indicating a preference isn't one that will define your career. Think about it carefully, of course, but don't be paralysed by worries about the future. You don't know which area of law – chosen by you or chosen by the firm – will be the one that makes you think, 'Yes, this is for me'. It might be an area you never expected to enjoy. Keep an open mind.

A brief impression of training

Next, let's get a flavour of training. Not day-by-day, but an overview so that we have shared context before we consider how you might approach matters as an individual in the rest of this book.

The first few weeks will be a blur of meeting different people – your cohort of trainees, the trainees above you, your supervisor, the colleagues in your new department, the people in the canteen, security. The list is long! You won't remember names. You'll almost certainly forget your pass in the first couple of weeks and stand wondering how you're going to get through a speed gate.

A month or so in, you know the people you interact with daily and the geography of the office. At this point you're comfortable you can get to (and in to) work and you know how to log on to the system. That's really all anyone expects by this point, because people know this initial period is hard. Bits of work have begun to arrive. (Ok, perhaps I'm underplaying it a little, but there will be a grace period during which you can establish yourself.)

Around three months in you're starting to get the hang of the work you've been asked to do. The skills you're learning are soft: how to research, how to present, how to draft emails and how to report to your supervisors/clients. You are not expected to get the right answer all the time, although clearly you need to try your best to reason tightly and answer appropriately, developing a professional approach. You begin to feel part of the team and have been to several events, with most departments having some kind of introductory social to welcome you and your contemporaries to the team. It would surely be rude not to.

At six months, just as you feel you're contributing usefully, it's time to move on. Having been allocated either to a seat you have requested or one selected by the firm, it will feel, either way, as though you're starting from scratch. From your perspective, the geography of the building will change, the work is different, the people are different, the demands are different. Don't panic. Everyone takes this first major change to heart. Remember, you are moving on with the skills you've learnt during the first six months without the burden of getting to grips with how the firm works.

It will feel strange – perhaps you are suddenly on an unfamiliar floor, the view from the window has changed, and new voices, bawling down the phone, disturb your concentration. But very soon that will, again, fade into familiarity and you will have grasped the essence of the work you're being asked to do. Enjoy the challenge. This, after all, is the point of training – to try different areas of law and to see what suits you, what sparks your interest.

We discuss supervisors in much more detail in Chapter 8, but for now it is enough to note that you will have a different supervisor for each seat, each with unique ways of working and specific requirements of you. How you might deal with those requirements is the subject of that chapter.

Second year: the next move, to seat three, should see a pay rise (always useful) and you've now been with the firm for a year. You have a better knowledge of its systems and have the measure of the people. During your

2 | WHAT DOES TRAINING LOOK LIKE?

third seat you should be comfortable in your trainee role and it will be much easier to get up to speed with a new area of work: you've done it twice before and you can relax into the pleasure of learning something new and navigating new personalities. People will know you're a third seat trainee and expectations will be higher than they were a year ago, so just be aware that the pressure may increase a little. You will be prepared for this. The year will have gone extremely quickly, and you may not recognise the experience you have gained, but I can assure you it's there!

At this point you will be able to reflect on the three areas of law you have so far explored. You may have a favourite; you may need to focus your attention on your fourth seat. We will consider how you go about making that final decision – where to qualify – in Chapter 12. Note for now that decisions will need to be made very quickly during your fourth seat and so you will need to be thinking about qualification throughout the process.

Seat three (or months 12-18 if you're on a six-month cycle) is a perfect opportunity to take a step back and reflect on what you have enjoyed and what you might like to achieve before the training period comes to an end.

As you move to your fourth seat the finish is in sight. At this point you are a truly helpful presence in whichever team you join, having at least 18 months' experience of the firm and its people. The pressure of moving will have dimmed, but the final seat brings its own concerns. If you have already decided where you want to qualify (and it isn't in the area of law practised in your fourth seat) this may feel like a difficult six months, your mind elsewhere.

In these circumstances try not to treat the experience as an afterthought; no knowledge is wasted, and it may be that the material you are exposed to and the contacts you make are helpful for the job you aspire to. For example, if you hope to join the corporate team but find yourself doing six months in commercial property, acknowledge that commercial property will be a crucial part of many corporate transactions. See the process as arming you for your future career, providing you with the tools to broadly identify (in this case) property issues, allowing you to get the right people involved when you become the lead corporate lawyer on a transaction.

Much of the talk during your final seat will be about jobs and, as I mentioned above, we'll look in more detail at the process of qualifying and applying for jobs in Chapter 12. At some firms a list will be published setting out the available roles for the qualifying cohort (the so-called 'jobs list'); at others, jobs may simply be offered. At some firms an interview is required; at others, the experience the firm has of your performance to date will be enough. It is unavoidable, given the perceived importance of the decisions made at this time, that rumours will fly and tensions will rise. Don't succumb to this. Try to ignore the inevitable noise.

In fact, this should be a calm time for you. By your fourth seat you have survived the challenges the training experience has thrown at you and you have (hopefully) identified an area of law that provides that special something for you – variety or work/life balance or extensive free-hand drafting or whatever has drawn you in.

Getting a job is hugely important; it is what you have worked towards for many years. Yet by this time all the hard work has been done. You will have dedicated yourself to soaking up all that you can about the area that interests you, ready for an interview and ultimately practice (and if you haven't, well, it's too late to change anything). You've kept in touch with the team you would like to join (see Chapter 12). You've worked cheerfully (see Chapter 5) and have built up a reputation and a great deal of goodwill around the firm. At this point you should feel confident in your future, regardless of the jobs position. You have survived and thrived.

Jobs lists tend to be published within three months of seat four (so during months 18-21 of the typical period of training). The timing will be similar if your firm asks for your preference rather than requiring a formal application. There must be sufficient time for interviews (if they are needed) and the administration of offering jobs in advance of the end of your training, hence the early start. No one wants any trainee to be disadvantaged, either by not getting the opportunity to apply for a job they want or by permitting the process to be circumvented, so ignore any talk about coffees with the senior partner dropped into conversation by the more overtly ambitious of your cohort.

Senior lawyers have spent time, and the firm has spent its money, on training you and ideally all trainees would be offered the jobs they want and stay at the firm. High retention rates – the percentage of starting trainees at a firm staying on, post-qualification – are a badge of honour. Clearly, however, the needs of the business will dictate the jobs that are available: that is something you cannot control and therefore shouldn't worry about. There may, unfortunately, not be a job in your chosen area which may make the last months of your training feel very long and rather disconnected from a firm you know you are leaving. Never fear. Speak to recruiters and see what is happening in the market. You will find the right role. We will discuss this further in Chapter 12.

On the last day of training there are likely to be drinks and nibbles with your colleagues. Some of you will be moving on to other things – other firms, other, non-legal, jobs. Many of you will be staying put, waiting only for the formalities of the Law Society and the SRA to change your email signature from 'Trainee' to 'Solicitor'. You should all be rightly proud of what you have accomplished. It's not an easy process, full of changing teams, changing work styles, changing areas of law. Your practising certificate will soon be with you. Well done!

Where do trainees fit? (Or, what is the hierarchy?)

Much is changing in law. At the time of writing, the profession is introducing new qualification routes, grappling with the implications of the (still new) SQE, and, in line with all other service industries as we considered earlier, facing changes to traditional modes of operating as hybrid working increases in popularity and availability. The advent of artificial intelligence adds a further complication, critical for law firms to deal with given the possibilities for automation of many of the process-based/form-filling and filing tasks lawyers do. Chapter 14 provides a brief overview of some of the predictions for the future of law.

Yet many things stay the same. Law remains a relatively traditional industry, and its emphasis on internal hierarchy is likely to persist whatever modernising the profession undergoes. Part of that persistence results from the very fact of the training model: having a defined 'trainee' position triggers a series of roles of increasing seniority governed by time. Let's run through the typical lawyer positions. Note that both the paralegal and solicitor roles can now be reached via apprenticeship schemes, the details of which may vary but the general experience will be the same as for those pursuing traditional routes into the profession.

Trainee: A book could be written about this role. (And you are reading it!) In short, someone who is less than two years into their legal career, fulfilling their period of recognised training, and all being well, qualifying as a solicitor at the end of this period. We know where we are with traineeship (or we soon will). Let's look at our colleagues.

Paralegal: Not on track for qualification as a solicitor but rather a standalone, fully formed, role. Paralegals are often legally trained and assist with administrative work under the supervision of either a senior paralegal or the lawyer whose work they are doing. In the UK, paralegals tend to have completed legal education and go on in most cases to undertake formal training as a solicitor or barrister. In the US, being a paralegal is seen much more as a career choice in its own right rather than a stopgap – and the UK is moving in that direction as more people choose to remain as paralegals and to develop the role. A paralegal who has remained in a team for a significant period and understands the work is invaluable to the business.

Solicitor: For some firms – but far from all – 'solicitor' is the designation given to the junior qualified cohort. This will capture newly qualified solicitors (NQs) through to around four years' post-qualification experience. Some firms refer only to 'associates' below partner level, but most distinguish in some way between junior and senior lawyers because it allows room for promotion rather more obviously. You might meet a 'senior associate', 'managing associate' or a 'principal associate' for example. These roles may, in turn, be hierarchical.

2 | WHAT DOES TRAINING LOOK LIKE?

The jump to solicitor from trainee is just beyond the scope of this book, but it is coming into view! It feels as though it's a big one: suddenly you are responsible for your work in a different way, no longer producing work for someone else to review and (often) develop in their name but instead a fully active member of the firm.

In truth, it is just another step on your journey, a subtle shift as you start to specialise in your chosen area of law, producing work of top quality, as you always have. The nature of the work will change. It will start as very similar to your trainee work, without the safety net of an immediate supervisor, but you will begin to explore delegation as incoming trainees assist you with tasks (just as you did, in your time) such as reviewing a data site, drafting ancillary documents, producing lease reviews and so on.

Associate: As you approach four years qualified (or so, it differs from firm to firm) you will be encouraged to apply for promotion to associate. As I mentioned earlier, it is frequently the case that qualifying trainees become associates immediately and stay that way unless and until they make partner. Here, I have broken down into the largest number of different categories I'm aware of firms regularly using so that you have an overview of the different designations used. No doubt there are further titles I haven't encountered!

Although promotion to associate tends to be by application, it is often a unilateral decision by the firm to promote you without need for an interview or business case (essentially, a function of time).

Associate solicitors are generally regarded as fully formed – happy to lead projects with support and sufficiently expert in their field that they need fairly minimal supervision. They are the powerhouse and, in most firms, represent a multiple of the seniors. So, you might have four associates to two senior associates to each partner. The client contact has increased considerably since you joined the team and at this stage (although in some fields a long time before) you may have your own clients or be responsible for a specific client relationship. If there are late nights to be done, you will do them here.

Senior Associate: Six to eight years post-qualification may see you offered the chance of further promotion, this time with an interview and often on the basis of an acceptable business case. At this point, you are a well-established lawyer, with the start of a reputation in your field. The promotion will be testament to your self-sufficiency although, as with everything in life, we carry on learning. You have particular client relationships that are considered helpful to the business, or you have the potential to create them. As mentioned above, there may be additional categories on the long road to partnership, such as a principal or a managing associate whose role in the department is sufficiently senior to be akin to a partner.

Professional Support Lawyer (PSL): Alternatively known as a professional development lawyer (abbreviated to PDL) or a Knowledge Lawyer, a PSL is an experienced lawyer who chooses a more academic practice. PSLs – as the name suggests – support their department, ensuring precedent documents are up-to-date, drafting papers responding to government and/or regulator consultations, co-ordinating internal cross-department meetings where there are changes that affect multiple teams and carrying out training.

PSLs are an invaluable resource, particularly when there are important and wide-ranging changes to the law. They have the scope and the time (it is built into the job) to focus on what is new and advise the rest of the team. They tend not to have client-facing responsibilities, so don't earn fees and don't have networking responsibilities as other seniors do.

Nevertheless, PSLs remain practising lawyers and at the forefront of the firm's intellectual/knowledge leadership efforts. They will represent the firm attending conferences and speaking at events, raising the firm's profile.

Legal Director (LD): Also known as Counsel. In some ways, this is the client-facing side of a PSL, and often an alternative to partnership. As an LD, you can maintain your client practice, but without the enhanced targets for generating work that come with partnership.

Legal Directors carry out work right across their departments and are often the people most interested in the technical side of the work. They may be excellent black letter lawyers (those who have a particular skill at legal drafting and the technicalities of legal issues), who are less interested in developing – and relentlessly pursuing – business leads.

That said, satisfied clients come back for more and LDs may end up generating an awful lot of work simply by being great lawyers.

Partner (salaried/equity): Should the day come when you are offered partnership, the rules surrounding that promotion will differ wildly between firms. For present purposes, it is sufficient to point out that there is usually a distinction between junior or salaried partners and equity partners. Salaried partners continue to receive a salary, have no profit share in the wider business and remain employees. So-called equity partners, as the name suggests, take a share of the equity of the firm and therefore co-own it and receive a share of the profits. The share of the equity changes over time, with the most senior partners usually being able to draw down the largest sums.

The intricacies of partnership are far beyond the ambit of this book – let's deal with being trainees first and not look too far ahead. Ambition is good but take it one step at a time.

I will say, as you might expect by now, the days have gone where partnership means you can put your feet up and leave it to the (senior) associates: taxing targets for bringing in work for the wider team are often in place and as clients become ever more savvy in their legal requirements, competition for work and a contraction in fees makes the balancing act at the top even harder.

Add to this the fact of managing a business – employees, new jurisdictions, office requirements etc – and the role of partner is clearly a pressurised one. It remains well compensated and is a challenging and rewarding job; one day it may be yours.

But that is a long way off. For now, let's consider how you fit in with your closest colleagues: paralegals and (junior) associates.

Most of your work will come from junior members of the team as instructions flow down through the hierarchy. This is useful because it means that you will be able to ask questions – the NQ lawyers will only be marginally ahead of you and generally willing to share their experiences.

You may come across junior lawyers who, because of their newly acquired qualified status, see themselves as very much your superior. That should never be the dynamic – you are a team. Still, the good thing in such a situation is that, although more work than you would like is delegated to you, you will get a vast amount of experience in a short time. And all experience at your level (indeed at any level) is a golden opportunity for development.

A word on paralegals as we leave this topic. As we have seen, law is a hierarchical profession. It is tempting to slot paralegals in a rung below you; to try to establish grades of colleagues; to palm work off on them. Avoid this at all costs. For a start, and as we have touched on, paralegals are permanently attached to a department and so are likely to be much more engaged in its ebbs and flows and the way it works – at this stage you are just passing through. They may be deeply experienced. That knowledge of the department means they will be able to help you with workflow, character updates, and, yes, pick up much of the administrative work that might be very time consuming for you.

You learn by doing, so only ever delegate something you have already done yourself and for efficiency's sake. Never delegate because you think it's something that's not for your 'grade'. Eventually you will be caught out.

Trainees: a vital part of the team

Why are trainees so important? Perhaps this isn't a question you've considered – it's just part of the process and we all go in at the bottom of a pyramid. Training is training.

There's truth to this, but it's certainly not the end of the story. Trainees are integral to the firm's structure. In law a price is put on your time. That price correlates to your level of experience indicated by the number of years you have been qualified or the amount of your traineeship you've completed – leaving aside, for now, complications such as fixed and capped fee arrangements which we will discuss in the next section.

2 | WHAT DOES TRAINING LOOK LIKE?

As you might imagine, you will be the cheapest legal resource in the firm (other than perhaps paralegals, although as many paralegals have extensive experience their time is frequently charged at a higher rate). But this means the firm can – and must – devote many more hours of trainee time than senior time towards an issue. The structure is built into the economics of law firms. You are an asset.

This is great news.

There's a tendency for trainees to worry that they are on the fringes of a department. You pass through quickly – even the longest seat of six months passes in a flash when everything is new – and on to the next thing. Everything you do is unfamiliar and so, however brilliant you might be, it requires effort and attention and takes you longer than you'd like. It may well be wrong, repeatedly.

But you should never think like this.

It's not an imposition to the wider team for you to be there. Quite the opposite. You are there because the firm needs you. More than needs you; this is the way it has chosen to undertake the work that it does.

Never worry that you are a burden. You are there to learn, to take time over things and to contribute what you can at the level you are at. Indeed, whenever you are asked to carry out some practical work such as compiling documents, undertaking searches, getting something printed, you (or your peers) are the people most likely to know how to do it. It will have been many years since a partner or senior associate dealt with putting documents on an encrypted drive or setting up repositories in the cloud – they don't know the firm's requirements. It's simply not cost effective.

In other words, you aren't surplus to requirements, watching and learning. This is on-the-job training, and you are fundamental to the system.

Why am I making so much of this? I know you are a confident lot; I've worked with trainees for years and without fail you are interested and switched on, ready to work. The fault I'm addressing isn't with you, it's with the system. In a high-pressure environment where you are regularly moving between teams it can feel – and other people can occasionally make you feel – as though your presence is at best unwarranted and at worst rather selfish and self-interested. This is simply not the case: you are a necessity of the business of law and any benefits which accrue to you are matched by those experienced by the firm. It is a reciprocal relationship and that's worth remembering.

(Briefly) Law as a business

Law is a business. It's a phrase you'll hear repeatedly when you join your firm; for those of you training in-house, the context will be different but the principle of increasing profitability by keeping down costs (in this situation you and your colleagues!) is equally applicable.

The fact that it's a common phrase is telling. Gone are the days (in most cases) of the trusted solicitor who becomes an irreplaceable advisor to a client. Generally, clients are shrewd: they don't want to pay by the hour; they don't want to pay for photocopying costs (seen as an overhead, a cost of doing business like any other consumable); they don't want to pay for internal meetings where work is allocated. This pressure increased after the financial crisis of 2008/2009 but was building long before. You will hear 'law is a business' often not because it's a general and meaningless truism but because after a glacial rate of change it *is* now a business rather than – as the profession historically liked to present itself – a set of staid advisors for whom cash was a dirty word and whose clients were charged on a consultancy basis.

The business of law is to provide legal advice and to manage legal risk. The costs to the firm will be its premises, its general overheads (services, consumables – imagine how much paper is used in a major law firm despite efforts to go digital) and first and foremost its wage bill. In a service industry, people are the product: the time cost of advice given by lawyers at a firm is what will ultimately be billed to a client. That will, of course, include the work that you do.

Income for law firms is generated by billing clients for the time taken on its projects by the lawyers employed by the firm. Lawyers at each grade (as we discussed earlier in this chapter) will be given a particular hourly rate. This has nothing to do with the qualities of the individual – it

2 | WHAT DOES TRAINING LOOK LIKE?

is standardised across the firm based on years of experience (and, occasionally, specialisms). As a first seat trainee, your billable rate may be in the region of £100 an hour; a senior London-based partner six or seven times as much. Again, there are any number of rates and billing structures across the profession, influenced by the type of work to geography. This is intended to be illustrative only.

Motivations for clients using law firms are complex. Individual clients could require everything from detailed tax structuring, setting up trusts for family money, to the attendance of a duty solicitor at a police station. Corporate clients might request relatively simple day-to-day support with an HR function in addition to much more detailed and intense advice when buying the shares of another company. Lawyers provide the advice they are qualified and competent to issue – as a trainee you are able to try out different areas of law under supervision. It is a privileged position.

Make no mistake, providing legal advice can be a risky business. By advising, lawyers are exposing themselves to claims that the advice given was incorrect or flawed. For this reason, lawyers are required to protect themselves by subscribing for professional indemnity insurance against claims from clients of negligence and other improper behaviour.

For clients, the expense of using lawyers is insurance of a kind. Should the lawyers advise negligently, the firm's professional indemnity insurance provides a potential safety net for loss-making decisions subsequently made, allowing the client to hedge its bets. It is, of course, also a cost to the business.

When a firm considers taking on a new client, it needs to be sure that it is able to do so from a conflict of interest perspective – at its most basic this is a regulatory requirement. Is the firm, for example, already acting for another party in the same project? Has it acted recently for the opposing party? If so, its duties towards those two separate clients will or may conflict. Crudely, there is a risk that the firm may not (or may be perceived not to) put its client's interests first. In such circumstances, the firm may not be able to take on the work unless certain safeguards are put in place. Note that this is a brief and necessarily gap-filled summary of a complicated feature of legal life, but hopefully you understand the point.

In a very small firm, discovering whether such a conflict does or might exist is likely to be quite easy: if the main solicitor isn't working on anything with the potential to cut across the proposed new client instruction, no-one else will be. In a billion-dollar firm, however, with hundreds if not thousands of lawyers across the globe, a sophisticated system of checks and balances is required to ensure the firm has a central, searchable record of its clients through which the existence or potential for such a clash of interests can be assessed. Producing such 'conflict' searches along with a first draft of a client engagement letter is a typical trainee role (and we will consider this further in Chapter 5). The specific scope of these procedures varies between firms. Just be aware that this is a sensitive and vital area of work despite being a routine occurrence pertaining to each and every client.

Reviewing potential conflicts is an intricate process, so much so that most firms will have a conflict committee of senior partners who can make decisions if a serious or high value conflict has arisen or is at risk of arising. If the conflict can't be appropriately managed, the work may have to be turned down. Even if it can be managed, is the proposed work likely to stop the firm (because of a future conflict) from taking on a different, more profitable project? Where does the balance lie? Conflicts management is a crucial part of the business although, granted, those decisions won't need to be made by you for some time. Just be aware of its importance.

When it comes to invoicing, a firm will look at the number of hours spent on a project by its lawyers, calculated in six-minute increments. We will examine the infamous six-minutes in Chapter 7, but the hourly rate for each grade of lawyer is clearly going to have to be set at a level such that both the overheads of the firm are covered and a level of profit is generated.

In theory, the firm is free to set these rates at any level; in reality it is much more nuanced. Market forces play their part – should an associate (who, invariably, will do much of the work) at one firm be billed at a huge sum, say £800 an hour, then that firm is likely to price out all

2 | WHAT DOES TRAINING LOOK LIKE?

but the clients with the deepest pockets and even those who can afford it are unlikely to want to pay, particularly if there is a good quality cheaper option elsewhere. So, there are the natural constraints of competition.

In a service industry, however, reputation has a significant role. So-called 'Magic Circle' firms – the five most prestigious firms in London – might charge a premium on the basis of their reputation for innovative and cutting-edge work. Similarly, the type of work can sometimes see an increase on standard rates: tax lawyers, for example, tend to regard themselves as particularly able (for reasons of complexity and a market willing to pay for them), and price themselves accordingly.

In the complicated interplay between these factors, we can also insert the resources and situation of the client. A client in financial distress may end up paying whatever is asked to get advice which it hopes will save its business; a secure multi-national with extensive experience of lawyers and legal frameworks may impose their own terms and rates, establishing competitive panels of legal advisors with remuneration dictated by the client. In such a situation, lawyers balance the benefits of (perhaps) a relatively low profit relationship against the profile that comes with dealing with some of the world's biggest business names.

Back to the invoice. Its amount will be, generally, at the discretion of the partner who is responsible for the matter but subject to various restrictions.

The starting point is the cost of time actually spent on the matter and any properly incurred disbursements (fees incurred by the lawyers on the client's behalf – so fees for barristers, fees for filing documents etc).

Second, the invoice will depend on what has been agreed with the client in the engagement letter (the terms agreed between a client and solicitor setting out what work is to be done and how much that work is expected to cost). Perhaps a 'time billed' basis has been agreed i.e. the amount of time recorded by each lawyer working on the project is added up, multiplied by their rate, and aggregated to achieve the final total. The most common alternative billing arrangements are what's known as a fixed fee arrangement, where the client is billed a set amount regardless of how much work is done, or a capped fee arrangement, where the client is billed what is 'on the clock' i.e. the time cost of the hours of work actually carried out, such a sum not exceeding an agreed amount. If you are working at a firm which obtains much of its income from the public purse, then there will be caps in place on what can be invoiced: turning a profit from such work is a delicate balance as very publicly discussed in the press.

Third, any further arrangement with the client agreed at the end of the engagement. It is often the case in corporate mergers and acquisitions work that the initial estimate of cost has been exceeded and a final negotiation will take place between partner and client on the reasonable mid-point between estimate in the engagement letter and the final time cost to the firm.

Law firms, like any other business, need to be alert to changing conditions in the market and to make sure that they are as insulated as possible against changes in the consumption of legal services. To do this, as you will no doubt have seen in the legal and national press, firms will sometimes merge with one another to create much larger entities, hoping that this will give them access to other markets and a wider range of clients. They will open offices in other jurisdictions around the world, with a similar aim of reaching new clients or taking advantage of favourable market conditions. They will open departments as developing legislation makes it necessary to provide clients with an additional or wider service. They will diversify into new avenues of work – increasingly possible since the late noughties where legislation permitted non-lawyers to own law firms for the first time and meant firms could benefit from external investment.

From your perspective, dealing with the business of the law firm is some way in the future. That's not to say it is something you can dismiss. For a start, particularly if you are going into a commercial firm (but useful wherever you train), considering the business model of your employer and how you contribute to it is likely to be a beneficial exercise. How is your salary generated and where do you fit into the future of that firm?

More immediately important, most firms want to know that you understand the firm as a business. Many qualification interviews are built

2 | WHAT DOES TRAINING LOOK LIKE?

around both your understanding of the area of law in which you want to practice and your understanding of the firm and its commercial options in the future. What avenues for new work or opportunities in other jurisdictions can you foresee?

The SRA, too, sees this as an important part of your knowledge acquisition. Although there is now no formal requirement to complete it, until 2015 newly qualified solicitors needed to undertake a management course devoted to, as the name implies, the management of a law firm and the balancing of lawyer numbers against fees to ensure profitability. The SRA no longer prescribes what is required to demonstrate, in its chosen phraseology, 'competencies to practice', but some knowledge of your business will clearly become necessary as your career progresses towards leadership.

Being practical

This is a whistle-stop tour through the business of a law firm, but a necessary one. As you move from the study of law to its practice, placing that practice in the context of commercial reality will give you an important alternative perspective. It's not about simply opening a book or web page and copying out an answer; it's not even about being the 'best' lawyer (whatever that may mean). It's about giving a practical answer to a paying client, making sure they see some value in the money they are spending.

Word of mouth recommendations remain a vital way in which people choose lawyers and so reputation is crucial. A lawyer's ability to work with clients, personably, is often paramount (see Chapter 10). You'll see this manifest itself, rather euphemistically, in descriptions of a particular lawyer or firm as 'commercial' or 'astute'. A key element is, of course, legal skill, but much of a lawyer's reputation is engendered when the client walks away saying, 'Yeah, I'd work with them again. They got me where I wanted to be and made that as painless as they could…and the fees made sense to me.' Being wise to that feeling will help you to be a better lawyer in the long-term, I guarantee it.

Takeaways

» A typical period of training at the time of writing is two years in length, with most divided into four seats of six months each. Moving seats can be difficult to begin with but eases over time and with experience.

» As you progress through that two-year period expectations will rise. Don't worry about this; your skills will develop, even if you don't notice it.

» Remember that a client is looking for a sensible response to a problem – they are paying for guidance and, if possible, resolution. It's not always about giving a forensic legal answer at length, but rather one that fits the client's brief.

» Pay attention to the commercial reality within which your firm operates and learn as much as you can. It impacts on your salary and how clients engage with you.

3 | THE FIRST DAY

The first day in any job is a series of contrasts: fear of the unknown but exhilaration at finally getting started; primed to work, yet having to sit through the enforced idleness of an induction process; meeting what seems like hundreds of people and not remembering a single name. It is a watershed – a before and after, where nothing is ever quite the same. One morning you are simply you, that evening you are an employee. Day two has nothing like the same resonance – from that point onwards you are off and running, a member of the team.

In this chapter, I want to discuss the first day. This book is all about managing expectations and it's important to know, on the first morning, the sort of things you can expect. Knowing what is coming, even in general terms, lets you relax into the moment and concentrate on making friends or soaking up advice or just trying to look as though you belong, however you're feeling inside.

Before we look at what the format of the first day might be, it's important to take a moment to reflect. What should you be thinking about in advance of those first hours and days?

Early thoughts

Confidence is clearly top of the list. You've earned your place: academically, through performance at interview, by your continued commitment to the role. Each of your cohort will find something difficult, different for each of you. Consider yourself part of the next generation of lawyers; in a very real sense the current senior lawyers are caretakers of the business for you. So don't be afraid to show enthusiasm for a long-term career at the firm. It's 'when I qualify', not 'if'.

We will discuss confidence time and again because it is something that regularly comes up when I speak to current and former trainees – 'I wish I'd been more confident'. Don't confuse this with over-confidence, arrogance. Being confident in the manner we are describing is to be centred, to be self-possessed. Feeling able to ask questions when you need to and making decisions when required. Being courteous to everyone you meet. It is the opposite of the brashness that an exhortation to 'be confident' sometimes implies. For now, just focus on your right to be part of the world.

Be flexible. If you take nothing else from this book, remember this: every person, every team, every firm likes to work in a slightly different way, and flexibility is therefore greatly prized. You will be carrying out a delicate balancing act of, on the one hand, working out how *you* like to work and the work *you* like to do against, on the other, fitting in with the contrasting demands of the individuals and teams you encounter.

Similarly, you will need to work consistently, in line with the house style of your firm (i.e. the general way in which documents and emails are presented), and at the same time adapt your presentation to the needs of a given client or supervisor. Don't be thrown by this – it is part of the challenge of being a modern lawyer and makes the role interesting – but do be alert to these tensions. The more flexible you can be, the more you can attempt to please both yourself *and* those you work with, although 'attempt' is the operative word here; you should already know that you can't please all people, all the time.

It is never too early to start thinking about client development (or business development as it's also called, rather snappily shortened to the phonetic 'bisdev' or the initials 'BD'). The trainee experience is the beginning of your career – a period of learning, of course, but you should start to think about ways to shape your future from the outset. Networking will be part of the job as you become more senior. Partners have targets for the amount of work they bring in and they do this through a web of contacts developed over time. Start to think about your approach to networking and, in the longer term, establishing those contacts: what works for you? Are you most at ease at sporting or social events – a cycle ride/an annual dinner? Are you more inclined to the cerebral side? You could meet

3 | THE FIRST DAY

(potential) client representatives at training sessions, ultimately presenting to them. There may be personal contacts you can utilise, friends from student life or those in other fields you meet during your training days. They will become more senior in their organisation as you grow in yours, so keep in touch.

Relax into professional life. It's a difficult line to tread, being relaxed enough that you can think clearly, that you are approachable and pleasant to be around, without appearing insouciant, 'chill' (and not in a good way). Take your cue from the team. This is a professional environment. Feet on the table won't give the right impression. In certain teams it will be perfectly acceptable to put on headphones and listen to music, especially in open plan offices; in others it will be frowned upon. Beware of over-familiarity. Read the team culture.

Spend some time thinking about the type of work you want to experience. This will, of course, be governed by the type of work your future firm carries out but, within that predetermined ambit, what aspect of practice do you want to experience most? In the corporate world, my background, a range of departments – and departments within departments – deal with everything from due diligence (the investigation into the 'health' of a company or organisation for sale) through to corporate tax. Within a commercial property team there may be sub-teams which deal with property litigation, planning, corporate support, residential property, commercial property. Researching via the firm's website the many sub-departments it houses and thinking about what sounds interesting is a natural place to start. Further research may be required to understand what 'property litigation' involves, but a search of the term will give you an overview.

Going into the process with an idea of the experience you would like to gain is helpful, although by no means required. Many people are simply happy to be joining the profession and have no particular view about the work they want to undertake beyond that headline decision of going to a 'corporate' as opposed to, say, a 'criminal' firm. Always keep an open mind: I went into my training contract convinced that my preference was a niche area of law which I could attempt to master. As it turned out, I much preferred the wider, more expansive role of a transaction lawyer. You just don't know what you will like until you get to try it, so don't be dogmatic.

From a practical perspective, attire is an interesting one. Many firms now operate a 'dress for your day' policy which means, as it suggests, how you dress should depend on what you have going on that day. If you don't have client meetings which (may) require you to dress smartly, you dress for your office which may mean smart casual, may mean downright casual, it will depend where you work. If indeed you're in the office – clearly, remote working days bring their own comforts. There are no strict rules anymore. A client meeting may not require a suit; the office may require a shirt. The only advice one can give is: be sensible. You want to look presentable while bringing some element of personal style. That's a well-being point, and an important one. You want to be able to bring your true self to work, albeit a true professional self.

There you have it. Beyond anything else you learn in this book, try to remain confident, flexible, relaxed, sensitive to opportunities to engage with clients and open-minded, curious, about the work. Above all, make every effort to retain a sense of self. You will be swamped with suggestions for different ways to work, required to make decisions, encouraged to succeed under pressure and pulled out of your comfort zone. You will do this best, and enjoy yourself most, if you pay attention to your preferences. How can you play to your strengths?

We will address all these things again in the context of work (Part 2) and people (Part 3), but they are core general principles to keep in mind from the very first day.

Walking in

This is the first day of a career you have spent many years working towards. How will it shape up? What will happen? How will you feel?

The first thing to say is it's ok to be nervous! This is 'first day of school' syndrome and – just like your parents said with that first school day, way back when – everyone else will be just as nervous. Well, most will be. In

3 | THE FIRST DAY

every group there's someone who is, or appears to be, immediately comfortable in every situation. They're ready to answer every question and know all about the world of law before having started, acting as a general irritant to you, your group and the people leading your introductory sessions.

In fact, this person is a great help – embrace them! There's nothing so awkward as the sound of silence in the face of a relatively simple question that the room declines to answer out of shyness, nobody willing to volunteer a thought. Someone to keep questions moving works in everybody's favour. Perhaps having read this book, you will be the one ready to contribute, given your knowledge of all things trainee related. I hope so. Just be sensitive to the ego of others.

Nerves are good. The rush of adrenaline you get as you walk into reception for the first time will help you sparkle. Just as in an exam where the answer comes, unexpected, from some unknown recess in your brain, that rush will help you. It will help as you meet security, saying your name confidently and clearly, and as you introduce yourself to your fellow trainees, ready to face the day.

Ranking equally with potential nerves should be excitement. As we recognised at the beginning of this chapter, the first day is a realisation of a long-held ambition – you wanted to become a solicitor and you're now one step closer to that achievement. The academic training is over and the real-world experience of life 'on the job' is now beginning.

You are becoming part of a profession full of interesting people with the brains both to carry out an enormously demanding job and to understand that there is much more to a rewarding and exciting life than law. You should be very proud of where you are and the decisions you have made!

Illustrative timetable

So, to that first day. Make sure you know exactly where you're going – where the office is, who you ask for on arrival, and anything you need to bring with you. Most larger firms have a dedicated trainee on-boarding team, and they will be in touch with you well in advance of your start date with this information and, very likely, a timetable of events for your induction. If your firm has not done this, you should get in touch with the HR representative (as set out in your offer letter) at least a month before you're due to start so that you are comfortable you understand the plan for starting.

Although each firm does it differently, in very general terms a first day timetable might look something like this:

Coffee to start: Coffees (or tea if you prefer) will become an integral part of your trainee life, covering (euphemistically) everything from a chat with other trainees, an appraisal, a deal debrief through to client encounters. Your first day will almost certainly open with a hot drink and a chance to meet your fellow trainees. They will be your support system. They are the ones who will come closest to understanding your experience, so meet and greet like hell.

An introduction to the firm and the jurisdiction(s) in which it operates: You will probably already know this, but it makes sense for the induction team to provide an up-to-date position, including any recent office openings, new (major) personnel hires, proposals for the future, giving you a snapshot of the firm at the time you join.

An admin session: There will need to be an hour or so devoted to handing in right to work documents (usually your passport or residency documentation), copying degree certificates, getting ID cards to access the building and any other first day administrative requirements.

A talk from the senior partner (of the firm or the office): This is the big boss or, at least, one of two – there is often a managing partner too, whose role is more internal and less outward-facing. The talk is a courtesy to welcome a cohort of new trainees and an opportunity for the person at the top of the firm to describe in very broad terms how your experience is intended to pan out; a commitment, of sorts. Of course, reading this book will have provided you with a good idea already, but at this point you will be given an individual overview of how your firm intends the relationship to work.

3 | THE FIRST DAY

Lunch: Something communal so you can continue to meet people, including trainees in the cohorts above you.

Meeting your first supervisor/'family': It is usual to have an introductory meeting with your supervisor. They may be busy, so if they don't attend, don't take that as a personal rejection (although it's certainly bad form).

Assuming they attend, they will introduce themselves and let you know what sort of work they are currently involved in and where you will be able to assist.

Some firms operate a 'family' system, a bit like those operated at many universities, where a trainee in one of the cohorts above will act as 'parent'. If your firm operates this system, you should also be introduced to your mentor on the first day. They will be a compelling source of information, not just about the characters at the firm, but also about opportunities for involvement in corporate social responsibility initiatives (known as CSR and including a multitude of chances to volunteer) and general advice about how they dealt with their early seats.

A legal session: Not all firms will do this, but some might have a session on the substance of being a lawyer. This should include taking you through the firm's house style, its client list (in terms of type/sector) and other firm-specific approaches to its legal work.

An IT session: This might not take place on the first day, but at some point quite soon after your start date there will be an IT induction. This is crucial, leading you through the bespoke systems the firm uses including its form of DMS (document management system) and time recording software. These are the tools you need to operate day-to-day so, if not included in your first day sessions, it will probably be the first thing you do on day two. This may not be as simple as it sounds. There are multiple programmes to learn, often interlinked, meaning that entries have to be made in a certain order. The exemplar is client on-boarding procedures, where the conflict searches that we discussed earlier in the chapter must be completed before anything else as they feed through to the systems for opening projects if that would-be client is taken on. You don't have to master everything all at once. As with any software, it helps to use it in earnest. Take notes and ask questions. Large firms with – perhaps – more complicated systems will have 'how-to' guides that you can access from the cloud and an IT development team to field any questions.

Welcome drinks: If you're lucky, the day will end with a glass of wine or a soft drink and some further networking with your cohort, other trainees and probably most of the junior end of the organisation. The hard bit is done; now the work begins.

What then?

At the end of Day One, the nerves of the morning will have evaporated, the building will be familiar and you'll have made the acquaintance of potential new friends. By the end of the first week, you will feel as though you have never been anywhere else. From this point onwards time speeds up and your training will accelerate towards its end point; qualification.

Much of this book is concerned with how to get the most from your training. We should take a moment to reflect on how great it is to be a trainee.

Most law firms are hugely social places, full of bright people with interesting ideas about the way they work and the work they do. As a trainee you are at the heart of the social side of the firm – organising events, getting involved in CSR and the activities of local law societies, taking part in training, competing in inter- and intra- firm sports events.

You have the freedom of the firm! Your movement between teams makes you the life blood of the organisation, carrying information and updates between groups that are otherwise separate fiefdoms.

You have a peer group! Don't underestimate this. Over time, people from your cohort will move on to other teams, other firms, other walks of life. Yet for the duration of your training you have a group of people of a similar age going through the same immediate experiences – in other words, built in support.

In actively learning and participating in legal life, you are supporting the lawyers you work with. You can extend your responsibility in line with your interests. Clearly there's a baseline below which your competence can't be allowed to drop and a ceiling to your assistance (you won't run projects alone), but discovering and following your passions is part of the process.

For the rest of this book we will consider in detail the challenges you may face, how best to prepare to face those challenges and the successes you can achieve. But remember, for all the reasons above, this is a fantastic time in your career and one I want you to be really excited about. Not just because it's an achievement to reach the milestone of 'trainee' but because of the kinetic potential built into the role. It really is an electric, exhilarating time, with opportunities which you can mould as you want. Lean in, as they say, and enjoy yourself.

Takeaways

» Be confident, flexible, keep a sense of self (how do *you* like to do it?) and give some thought to what area of law you want to experience in advance of starting your training. There are no guarantees, but thinking about what interests you is never wasted time and allows you to position yourself.

» Day One inductions will vary in substance. Don't try to remember everyone's name and everything that's said. Do make sure you take plenty of notes and get to know as many of your cohort as you can.

» Look out for your supervisor and a trainee-mentor (should you receive one). You will be working closely with them, so be attentive and enthusiastic. Quiz your trainee-mentor about the department you will join; this is perfectly acceptable and it's important to understand the characters in a team. Working with these people effectively goes far beyond anyone's legal abilities – how do they react to stress, to newcomers, to uncertainty? To holiday requests!

» Being a trainee is a genuinely exciting time. You have tacit permission to explore the offerings of the firm and local law societies. You have a peer group to do this exploration with. Take the work seriously but get involved in as much as you can handle. And, crucially, enjoy it.

4 | TRAINING WHEN TRAINING

In this chapter we will look at the importance of ongoing training, legal or otherwise, as distinct from your general experience as a 'trainee'. A clash of terminology, I know, but something we must learn to live with.

Having come through three or possibly four years of university, you might think that your academic life is behind you. To some, if not all of you, the end of exams may be a relief.

There is good and bad news.

The bad news is that the training stage is never over. Much as a doctor (or other professional) must constantly ensure their knowledge is as up-to-date as it can possibly be, that their skills are regularly honed and refreshed, a lawyer faces a continuing responsibility to update their knowledge and skill set. This obligation is both imposed by legal regulators and, much more importantly, necessary for carrying out the responsibilities of the role. Legal knowledge, crafted into suitable advice, is the product being offered; the service provided.

More than that, your firm will be trying to differentiate itself from other firms. To that end, training will (or should) go beyond legal knowledge and into any area where there are useful skills or knowledge to be adopted. This could include project management skills, writing skills, other specialised knowledge that is complementary to the area in which you practice. Although clients will take it as read that you have certain legal skills, being able to offer something more suggests a capability and dynamism that other lawyers in other firms may not have.

The good news is that the road to becoming capable and dynamic is one of exploration and discovery. Training, far from being something you drag yourself to, can and should be central to your working life. It can be interesting, it can be alarming, it can even be exciting.

The trouble is, it mostly isn't. It's mostly dry and/or feels irrelevant and/or you are the only person sitting in a room staring at some confusing slides and listening to someone in the Carlisle office (who has clearly never done a presentation before and models their style on the frenetic mumblings of an online conspiracy theorist). In this chapter we will explore why you should love training – and how it can do *everything* for your career.

Professional requirements

There are two aspects of the training experience for you to think about once the academic requirements are satisfied: the regime mandated by the SRA and, separately, the training offered by your respective firms and/or provided by external bodies that your firm deems (or you decide for yourself) will assist you in your practice.

The SRA prescribed training is picked up in the second stage of the Solicitors Qualifying Exam (SQE 2) or, for anyone who is still able to qualify via the LPC/training contract route, by way of a Professional Skills Course. The regimes are similar, looking at the practical elements of lawyering: client interviewing, advocacy, case/matter analysis and legal research, writing and drafting. Specific details of the regime are beyond the scope of this book. Full details can be found on the SRA's website.

One impact of the introduction of the SQE is that you are regarded, in theory, as having more responsibility for your training. If you have carried out training of the correct duration and passed the SQE, you will be ready to practice. It will be up to you to push for the experience you want in order to be ready to deal with clients on day one of your qualified life.

This is an opportunity, no doubt. It means that, if you really like a seat you could ask to extend beyond its allocated time because there is no external pressure to move on. This would, clearly, depend on the willingness of your firm to be flexible. Although the expectation is that most firms will stick with the tried and tested form of the training contract, there are bound to be changes to the ways in which firms operate as they push for innovation. You can be part of that process more actively than any trainees before you.

Internal training opportunities

Opportunities for training sessions within the firm is a different matter entirely. There's a great deal of flexibility. There's also a tension between ongoing training and the demands of client work; and with training frequently limited to legal updates, the incentive to attend – whether virtually or in person – diminishes.

Law firms aren't alone in failing to make training sessions the highlight of a week. Too often and in too many industries, they are viewed as a necessary evil, held in a lunch-hour for people whose desks heave with work to worry about. In the allotted time there's usually only scope to scratch the surface of a topic and the inevitable PowerPoint presentation is so meme-worthy it's beyond parody.

Much as we would like to, we can't change this (and hopefully it goes without saying that I'm being somewhat facetious – there will almost always be points of real value to learn). The challenge will be how you engage with the opportunities provided and how you use training to your advantage. And it will be an advantage: the breadth of your knowledge is frequently as important than its depth in a professional environment.

Let's consider the types of training available to trainees.

The most common: internal training run by colleagues in the firm. Participation in departmental training sessions will inevitably be a requirement for all members of the department you are in for the time you are in it. This may involve a presentation on a particular area of law or a particular project given by one (or more) of your team. This could be in conjunction with members of another team – the employment department giving an update to the pensions team, for example, describing pertinent recent developments that cross the practice areas.

Occasionally 'round table' sessions are organised to discuss a specific issue, a new piece of legislation perhaps. A true round table anticipates contributions from all, but it's more likely that sessions to which you are invited bearing this name will take the form of a discussion between two or three more senior members of your team, before being opened to the floor for comments. A variation on this theme is the regular team meeting, perhaps every two weeks, where legal issues can be discussed alongside general housekeeping for the team. There will be other examples.

From a practical perspective, especially for those of you who work in organisations with multiple offices and national or international reach, presentations can be difficult to follow. Online sessions in particular can be difficult to remain engaged with as disembodied, delayed voices and a static camera (often off!) may mean that it's tricky to follow who is speaking. This is exacerbated where the training takes place physically and you are dialling in as the exception. Most of your colleagues will not be natural presenters and although (perhaps because) the content is familiar to them, it is often difficult to get across to a captive audience the relevance of the points being made. That audience (you) will also have pressing work concerns and lunch plans which have to be put to one side to attend the training session, often impeding any significant learning.

External training opportunities

A very different experience – although suffering from some of the same issues – will be external training courses. Whatever programme is in place for trainees at your firm will vary immensely. The content is likely at this stage to be focused less on law (dealt with in-house) but rather on aspects of practice – advocacy if you are likely to be appearing before magistrates; the business world if your firm is heavily corporate.

In the recent past some firms developed bespoke MBA-style courses designed to introduce trainees both to the commercial world of most clients and to the overarching concepts of business within which law firms operate (although the attraction of this approach seems to have waned). These courses, too, suffer from the disadvantage of being packed into long days when you are almost certainly busy, with presenters who frequently read from materials, dynamism being a dirty word.

I am playing devil's advocate. Quite unfairly, I have characterised these sessions – and those offered internally – as painfully dull when in most cases presenters will have agonised over the content for weeks in advance and will try very hard to make it engaging. Further, many large firms have adopted an academy model, where training on myriad subjects with interactive graphics and professionally acted case studies are made available for you to pursue at a time of your choosing. My point is that, despite these efforts, training is often an after thought, and it shouldn't be.

Responding to training

You will have no control over the quality of the presentation, but you will have control over your response to it and any contributions you can make. What can you do to make sure training is relevant? Or, put another way, how do you get the most out of it? I give some suggestions below.

Active listening and proactive questioning. Try to start conversations with seniors that attend. You are at the cutting edge now: the training is likely to be about some new aspect of the projects you work on – it's no longer theoretical. Senior lawyers are there to impart the wisdom of experience. And most love nothing more.

Ask questions, then or later after reflection. Note things that interest you and get you thinking. Perhaps counter-intuitively, this is most effective if the presentation is dull or hard to follow; write down some key points to follow up later and, if you're not engaged, use the time to consider who you might talk to about those one or two interesting points that emerge. There will always be a titbit that grabs you, so don't waste the opportunity to take something away.

Reflect on your own presentation skills. Getting up there and leading discussion will inevitably be part of your job at some point, whether it is presenting to colleagues or pitching to clients. What is the presenter doing that is making it so hard to follow? How could you present the same information in a more interesting way? What tools could you use? Various platforms have built whole businesses out of providing creative alternatives to PowerPoint. Could you include some well judged quotations from a great thinker or two? Work in a song title? Treating your subject with a bit of humour will make your audience grateful and keep them alert, much like changing your tone and volume. Clearly this requires judgement, a reading of the room and adherence to the guidelines put in place by your firm.

Don't try to take loads of notes unless that is how you work naturally. Some people, and I am one of them, like to scribble everything down as it helps me to process what's being said, but that's not true of everyone. If that's not your working style, you risk getting lost in piles of paper (or OneNote records as the case may be). Instead, try to keep a record of key points. You might keep a training journal or a folder with the handout and a couple of paragraphs of thoughts. Training is only ever an awareness tool. Should you ever need to apply the material you will need to research it and make sure that you understand the law as it stands when the question is asked, meaning you don't necessarily need lengthy notes. Just make sure you understand the key take-away points and the circumstances in which the issue might crop up.

Volunteer to be involved. This is tough. Even if you are a seasoned public speaker and nerves are non-existent, talking to knowledgeable people about the subject of their expertise is daunting. But this trepidation is precisely why it's such a useful exercise – preparing to speak to people about a subject compels you to learn about it in a different way. You are explaining, not regurgitating. Further, it is a requirement of most firms' internal training schemes that presentation skills are developed and assessed. This means you will be asked to give presentations to one (or several) of the departments you pass through – perhaps on a recent case, or some incoming legislation. In other words, presenting is part of the trainee experience and, subsequently, an integral part of your professional life. Embrace it. People will be kind and will appreciate your enthusiasm.

For external courses, take advantage of what is offered. You don't know where you will end up on qualification and if external training opportunities – rare and expensive – are offered, then avail yourself of them. If you find a course that is interesting and pertinent but not something considered as part of the trainee role, there's nothing to stop you requesting to attend. You might need to make a business case – perhaps you could offer to feed back to the whole department by way of a presentation? Two birds, one stone.

Underpinning all of this are the continuing professional development (CPD) requirements of the SRA. Although CPD won't be a concern for you as trainees (trainee life being almost all development), regular CPD is important in your qualified life and good habits are best made early. At the time of writing, the SRA takes a competency-based approach, requiring solicitors to self attest that they have kept their knowledge and skills up to date rather than mandating (as used to be the case) a certain number of hours of CPD be completed. Therefore, thinking carefully about the type of training you might do is built into the professional role.

Impact on your career
How will this help you in your career? Although almost all lawyers in the modern system specialise in a particular area of law, the skill of a great lawyer is in recognising connections, joining the dots. If you're acting in an employment matter, the additional skill is recognising the related corporate issue and either dealing with it if you are competent to do so or, more likely if you are in a larger firm, involving a colleague who specialises in that area; if you're acting in a family matter, recognising the personal tax issue and, again, taking steps to move that issue on. Getting used to regularly attending training and, by virtue of that, becoming attuned to finding connections rather than acting in a self-contained bubble, will help you to become a much better lawyer. Your legal knowledge increases as the soft skill of piecing together legal information develops.

Maybe this reads a little defensively. 'Of course,' I hear you say, 'training is crucial. I'm a student, have been for years, and I expect training in order to learn!' The trouble with – and the joy of – professional life is that you're learning all the time, on the job, and it often feels as if there's not enough time for anything else. The common refrain from people of all levels is that they're 'too busy' for training – mandatory or not – but in my view that takes it all too literally. Yes, the training itself is useful, but more important is making space for the *habit* of training. Making that time available, regularly, to be part of a conversation about what is going on in the field/the department/the firm brings all sorts of benefits: enhancing the team experience, people learning from people, the meeting (albeit often virtually) of geographically separate teams, awareness-raising of key issues. As a trainee it also gives you the psychological boost of making you feel as though your development matters to the team.

So soak it all up – go to all the training you can. Depth of knowledge will come later, once you have decided where you want to qualify. For now, the range of your experience (including training) is the important thing. It will not be wasted time.

Takeaways

» Training is a fact of life. Continual learning about your chosen area of law and where it fits into the wider schema of legal practice is a requirement of modern lawyering.

» Both internal and external opportunities will present themselves. Take advantage of as much as you can.

» Presentations may, on occasion, not be very good. Avoid switching off – take notes of an interesting point or two to discuss with your wider team or supervisor.

» Actively engage. Ask questions. Ask for stories and experiences from seniors and those offering the training.

SEAT 1: COMMERCIAL LITIGATION

'STARTER FOR TEN'

A note on Alex and her journey

You might think it strange to find fictional interludes in this book, but they have purpose. In preparation for writing the book – talking to trainees, former trainees (which of course is everyone in the profession), and those currently acting as supervisors – I heard many views on the trainee experience. Those views came with narrative context: stories about work that went well, experiences enjoyed, jobs that became nightmares, things people wished they'd known 'when I started'. Advice distilled from those conversations fills the pages of this book, yet it felt like something was being lost.

The trainee experience is multi-faceted, a product of the interplay of personalities (yours, your supervisor's, the members of your team), the type of work carried out, the number of other trainees, the matters in play during your time in a department and, as we will see, the weird and (sometimes) wonderful side projects you are catapulted into. These factors come into play simultaneously, overlapping to create the training experience. Only with that context is the full story told. Capturing a trainee's experience from start to finish – albeit fictionalised – takes us under the skin of training in a way that a description of its constituent parts cannot.

And so we follow the adventures of Alex. She has completed the prerequisites for training and is undertaking a standard training period of two consecutive years at a mid-sized law firm with a corporate/commercial bent. Her training is divided into four seats: commercial litigation, planning, corporate and a secondment to a client. Other than that, she (deliberately) doesn't have an established back story. Her background is yours, or someone very like you, using a little imagination. We will stay with Alex throughout her two years, each interlude a seat, following the challenges she experiences and celebrating the successes she finds.

For some of you, the corporate/commercial base won't reflect your experience. But Alex must work somewhere and, as no operation that I know of dabbles in *every* area of law, a corporate/commercial background is convenient as it reflects my own. Even so, the choices she faces and the efforts she makes to succeed are reasonably generic and should permit you to visualise the experience.

A note of caution: the interludes are both fictionalised and intended as a bit of light relief, so don't hold Alex up as an exemplar of a trainee or rely on her story as a guaranteed description of a training contract – far from it. Each trainee's journey is different, and Alex takes a singular route, all her own. In watching how someone else does it, I hope it brings home some of the advice given so far; certainly, if you look for a lesson or two from each part of this book you will find it.

Considering your approach to the profession in advance is the point of this book. The illustration of experiences with colleagues, with clients, encountering matters outside the norm, will enable you – I hope – to think about how you would react to similar challenges in the context of *your* personality, *your* training and *your* firm.

Onwards, then, to the first seat, where Alex learns that her seniors are only human and to trust her instincts.

SEAT 1: COMMERCIAL LITIGATION

In which Alex learns to fight her corner.

'Not bad; not bad at all.'

Alex tried to hold back a smile and couldn't.

'Keep it up.'

Nathan was back from holiday and Alex, unsure if he would be relaxed having been on a beach for two weeks or under the dark 'back to the office' cloud, had been waiting with bated breath for some indication of whether the first piece of work had been a success. It had taken time. Two hundred pages of research reduced to a carefully worded ten-side summary. She'd even looked on the internal system to find a format and those ten neatly tabulated pages read all the better for it. Ok, it wasn't Shakespeare (what is?), but she'd been happy with her efforts and was pleased that Nathan seemed to take the same view.

During induction – between sessions on the firm's IT systems, a seminar on dictation, at least an hour on how to position her chair, and a drinks meet-and-greet with her fellow newbies and the other trainees (no guesses which was the most informative) – Alex heard that Nathan could be a difficult supervisor: that he liked things to be done in very specific ways, that he could be blunt verging on rude, even that he had made a previous trainee cry by criticising work. It put Alex on edge, but, a people-person, she was generally confident that she could and would win anyone over eventually. Anyway, there was nothing for it but to hold one's nerve, meet him and do the best she could.

In the end, it was a gentle opening to their working relationship. Two weeks of induction (just trainees and trainers) and a further fortnight with Nathan away on business meant that Alex didn't receive work from him for the first month. Month two saw some action – primarily the research summary – but Nathan's holiday to the lakes meant he'd read nothing. She wasn't idle and there had been plenty of work from other people in the department, but it felt a bit removed. She figured it would be sensible to get some feedback. And he'd liked it!

Nathan put the papers on her desk. She could see red pen, changes to be made, but the overwhelming feeling was relief: that she could hold her own and write something sensible. As a rule, she didn't worry about these sort of things; work is work, you do your best (or more accurately what you can) and move on. But there's something about starting at a place where everyone around you has been working towards the same thing, been through the same rite of passage. There's a measuring up that's inescapable.

Alex suspected everyone felt that way, at least she very much hoped they did. Confidence comes with time. Still, getting the first major piece of work in a fairly good state was a start she would happily take. 'Highly strung' Nathan seemed to have stayed away and she allowed herself to relax a little; perhaps, she thought, I'm actually good at this.

Days later Nathan had further news.

'I've spoken to Grad Recruitment and they'd be happy for you to extend this seat if you'd like? I know you're meant to go on to tax and it's entirely your choice, but I think you've made a great start here and I'd really like you to hang about for a bit. Let me know when you've had a chance to think about it.'

This time, she didn't try to stifle the smile. At lunch, she mentioned it to her mentor – Andreas – and his fellow second-year, Carla. Neither of them had heard of this happening before, which made it an even better proposition.

'It's massively flattering,' she told them, 'but I don't want to accept just because of the compliment. It's meant to be a split seat: 3 months each of commercial litigation and tax. Missing out on the second bit might be an advantage, right? I might actually get to grips with litigation proper rather than knowing a very little about both.'

'It's up to you, totally, but I can see it'd be difficult to turn down,' was Andreas' view. 'And a bit tough to carry on working with him when you've opted to move on!'

'I really don't think that's true,' Carla told them. 'I mean I completely agree that it's your choice (of course), but he can't take it personally. It's an offer, right? What if you had your heart set on tax?'

SEAT 1: COMMERCIAL LITIGATION

They all smiled at how unlikely that seemed.

'In fairness, I did want to see what the tax world was all about,' replied Alex, 'but I can live without it as long as it doesn't put anyone's nose out of joint.'

Carla didn't mince her words. 'They're not going to care whether you come or go in tax. The decision's yours. Don't let it influence you, but I've heard that tax is a bit of a slow burner: things are so complicated there's relatively little you can do as a total newcomer, let alone in three months. It'd be very much a taster.'

'Interesting. I'll have a think,' Alex told them. 'Anyway, drinks on Friday?'

***

Friday Pub had been a tradition at the firm for as long as anyone could remember, but that's also as far as it went – a day and a place. A small room at the top of the office became, for an hour or so after four on a Friday, a small 'pub' serving beers, lukewarm wine and soft drinks. The social committee put great emphasis on the different events it organised – gone were the days that everything revolved around drinking – but Friday Pub held a special place in the firm's heart. Well attended, it provided an opportunity to see people from other departments, especially important for the new trainees, six weeks in and with much to discuss.

Top of the agenda this week was a story from a legal gossip blog about a disastrous client event at a competitor – a South Downs electric scooter ride which left several people needing medical attention and one partner having to shave what was left of his hair – which Andreas told at the top of his voice.

In the stunned silence that followed, Alex found a moment to mention the proposition. The feedback was mixed: that she would blow any chance she had of qualifying to litigation if she turned the offer down; not progressing to the tax seat would damage her credibility within the firm; graduate recruitment had a fearsome reputation, could and would put a black mark by her name limiting her future choices; that it was an opportunity not to be missed and she had obviously smashed it (contributed rather insincerely from Mo, the paralegal who, he told everyone, was only treading water and was definitely going to be a barrister).

The most helpful advice came from one of the legal directors, overhearing the conversation as she reached for her orange juice.

'It won't matter to anyone but you – just make a choice based on the work not the people. If you're enjoying it, want to learn more, and can put up with Nathan, stay put. If you want a new challenge, move on.'

The conversation turned to the Christmas party. Despite it being mid-September, emails from the committee were already coming thick and fast: save the date; change the date; choice of food; revise the choice; revert to the original choices and only email back if the choices have subsequently changed. Andreas was unconvinced.

'I'm looking forward to it, but it's a bit of a shambles.'

'On the committee then?' Alex asked – in all innocence.

'Well no, but how hard can it be to get the right date.' Andreas bristled. 'On or around the middle of December, right? I thought these things got booked as soon as the last one finished.'

Carla, who had unwittingly accepted a planning role for the previous year's departmental Christmas 'do' (the presidentship of various clubs at university weighing heavily in her memory) had much to say on the subject.

'Don't get me started. No-one wants to organise these things and when someone finally volunteers, produces a tentative plan, gets it signed off by the rest of the committee (half of whom will miss all the meetings) and publishes it, all anyone can do is complain. No, you either go into these things with your eyes open and do it your way – and if you want a Spice Girl theme then good for you – or you steer clear. It's a disaster, start to finish. An utterly thankless task.'

'So, do we know anyone on this year's committee?' Alex asked, laughing.

'Maybe,' Carla said, looking away.

* * *

SEAT 1: COMMERCIAL LITIGATION

Two days later, Nathan seemed to be in a particularly good mood. The announcement of a successful application for summary judgment on behalf of a long-standing client flooded the floor with an irresistible aura of delighted professionalism.

'It's the second coming!' a shout, from the end of the office. 'Like when Prince changed his name to a symbol; you're coming out from under the stairs!' Alex took the pop culture as a sign that now might be a good time to broach the issue. In any event she was, hopefully, going to add to his good day.

'I'd love to stay on, if you still think it will be ok with grad recruitment?' she told him, as he wandered back to her end of the office.

'Great news! I'll give them a call at some point this week – it was already agreed in principle. I think you'll get more out of the longer placement and I've been really impressed with the work you've done so far. We can talk about qualification as well. Down the line.'

As Alex wandered back to her desk, a small part of her wondered whether his enthusiasm was misplaced. The first piece of work was something that she'd understood, been given a lot of time to complete (albeit by a quirk of fortune) and she'd discussed it with other members of the department before Nathan returned. It didn't mean – she knew – that she was the genius Nathan seemed to think she was. One good piece meant nothing; it could just be beginners' luck. But then, as she'd read, no-one is immediately a brilliant lawyer; a prodigy in the first month of practice. It just doesn't work that way. She knew from the trainee guide she'd read before starting that so much of the day-to-day work is convention born out of experience: you need to learn the area of law you are working in; the key resources in that area; where to find those resources on the IT system of your firm; how to apply those resources in a business sensitive (or commercially aware) manner. None of that comes naturally.

Nathan must know that, Alex thought, and what else could she do but be pleased about the impression she'd made and the opportunity to experience in greater depth the work of the department? She put the doubts from her mind, or tried to, and went to buy Andreas and Carla a calming bubble tea. She liked Nathan, the team and seemed to be doing well. Anyway, she decided, putting the matter to bed, if you can't enjoy a day like that then there is no point in getting up for work in the morning.

* * *

Two months later and the decision was, Alex thought, perhaps an error. Nathan, it turned out, was acerbic, passive-aggressive and occasionally just rude. The note left on her chair that morning was an exemplar: 'Please review the filing for Traverse. It needs to be in place by 3pm. Failure to do so will be a career limiting move.' She couldn't understand what had changed.

The shift started when he'd asked her to produce a memo on some new legislation in advance of a client meeting. Alex knew that the other trainee in the department had been working on documenting the implications of the new Act since they'd joined the department (almost four months ago). He'd been sent to seminars, on training sessions and was tasked with keeping the relevant precedent documents up-to-date for use by everyone. His entire job was to get on top of this stuff. Plus, he was in his final seat and so had the full picture: he understood the resources the firm had and the material that might be interesting to the other lawyers. Alex had just started. She was a fast learner, she knew, but she was beginning to realise the value of experience.

It was 24 hours before the meeting and she'd given it her best shot. She'd taken one of the summary papers circulated round the team and summarised it further: a two-page crib sheet for Nathan to review before the meeting. She showed it to one of the associates in the department, Michelle, five-years qualified, kind eyes, sharp mind, who liked the use of house style and said it captured the essence of the legislation.

But to Nathan it was useless.

She wasn't sure what he'd wanted although, in fairness, she hadn't asked – he always seemed too busy and the tone of voice when he'd asked her to produce the work was so final that she felt she couldn't reopen the

SEAT 1: COMMERCIAL LITIGATION

issue. The timeframe he'd given also suggested it only needed to be short. The scope of the new Act was vast, impacting every part of the department's work and a day and a half was barely enough for her to print out some high level commentary from the system, let alone digest and regurgitate it on paper.

'There's no detail here Alex – and no analysis whatsoever. I was going to use this to walk the client through the upcoming changes, but your note doesn't really even spell out what they are, let alone any impact for the business. It's too late now to do anything – you might as well just go home and we can talk about this at appraisal time.'

Since then there'd been little improvement. Every piece of work she did seemed to irritate him more. At first, she thought she could rectify the situation. At school, at university, she'd prided herself on her ability to cross divides and get on with everyone. But the more she tried, the harder it got to keep things civil, let alone impress. The nadir came when Nathan asked her to check a copy of a document.

'Could you go over this for me – I need to know that they match exactly.'

He dropped on her desk a hard copy file recalled from document storage with two post-its tagging the relevant pages.

By this point, Alex was so nervous about doing work for him that even copy-checking made her edgy. She skimmed the two short passages, confirmed the match, and moved on to do some work she could actually enjoy: a letter for Michelle, part of an ongoing dispute. Michelle had a completely different style of working. She was collaborative and positive, preferring to work together to produce something rather than taking Alex's work and using it (or not) without further comment – Nathan's approach.

Alex found working that way really inspired her. She felt she learnt much more by working through drafts and listening to the comments Michelle made; small things, like consistency of terms, fonts, formatting, pointing out errors by indicating where she might need to do further research rather than just giving the answer. It was constructive and rewarding.

'This is wrong. Again.' Nathan loomed over her. 'I've spotted two words that are missing in the copy. Please check it again. I'm sorry, Alex, but I won't be able to give you work if this is the standard.'

Her face was scarlet.

'Try taking it to one of the meeting rooms and reading it aloud.'

She did as he suggested, her stomach in knots. She knew she was trying, but every mistake seemed to justify Nathan's doubts. What made it worse was that her work for other people seemed to be good; perhaps, she wondered, they were just being kind to her? Maybe she wasn't cut out for this.

There were three discrepancies in the document – she had no idea how she'd missed them. When she marked the changes and handed them to Nathan he gave her a long look, loosened his tie and pushed back his chair. She thought he was going to speak; he didn't. Instead, he lifted his glasses from the table and turned back to the computer. Later that day, he sent her an email scheduling their first appraisal for the following Monday.

* * *

On a Friday evening in a café that used to be a chapel – cosy booths, dim lighting – Alex told Carla how difficult it had become.

'I have literally no idea what to do. Every time he asks me to do something, I panic. I know it's going to go wrong and it does. It's so weird, because other people I do stuff for seem fine with my work.'

'Do you think it's just a personality clash?' Carla asked. 'Although, word on the street is that he's really difficult – we talked about it at the beginning.'

'It started so well. That's what makes it difficult to understand – and so embarrassing. I mean, I agreed to extend the seat! It's just so awful to feel that I'm terrible at this when I've been working towards it for so long. I know we all have, but…'

Seeing Alex close to tears, Carla jumped in.

'Tonight we need to forget it – you can't do anything about Monday and there's no point worrying about it until you know what he has to say. I think you need to speak up though and tell him how you're feeling.

SEAT 1: COMMERCIAL LITIGATION

Respectfully, I guess, don't say what you really think!'

Alex laughed at that, back from the brink. It's just a job, she thought, how bad can an appraisal be?

* * *

'Come on, let's head out and I'll buy you a coffee.' Nathan was smiling at her, glasses on his head. He looked somehow softer without them; warmer, less hawkish. Turning out of the office, right and right again, a coffee shop with a few seats outside. They sat and Nathan bought drinks. Silence for a moment.

'So tell me how you think it's going?'

Alex thought for a second and then decided it was best to air it.

'I'm enjoying it. People have said some good things about my work. I know we've had difficulties, but I'm really enjoying the work and the department.' She realised that was true, despite everything. Nathan looked at her and took a sip of coffee.

'I should start by apologising if you feel any of this has been personal. Um, it really isn't.' He paused. 'Part of the difficulty for me has been that we're not used to having first seat trainees in the department – as a rule we try and push for trainees in their second year. It's complex work and the newer trainees often make more of a difference in other departments where they can get involved earlier on. With you, I should have taken that into account. But your work was so good early on that I think we both got a little ahead of ourselves.'

Alex smiled at that. 'I think we also might have slightly different working styles.' She felt a little embarrassed saying that to him, after all, he was *the* professional who had been at this for years. Surprisingly, he looked pleased.

'I think that's perceptive of you. Certainly, much of the feedback I've had from others in the department suggests much greater consistency, perhaps greater quality than you've shown me. I know I can be bad at giving feedback, but I really expect my trainees to pay attention to detail.

I feel like yours is getting worse rather than better.' It stung.

'I find it difficult to concentrate on the work you give me. I don't think you'll be pleased with the outcome and, I guess, panic a little. And I don't always understand what it is you want me to do.'

Again, Nathan hesitated, finding the words.

'I appreciate it's a lot of pressure, but that is part of the job. There are ways of coping. You can take work somewhere you can concentrate – one of the breakout rooms or the coffee bar – if that helps. Talk it through with one of the juniors. They're busy, but they'd be happy to talk to you about it; they've all been there themselves. As for understanding what you need to do, I'm very happy to discuss it with you, but you need to be very clear about what is confusing you and what advice you need. We can have a weekly catch up if you think that's helpful?'

Alex was surprised – and pleased – with how responsive Nathan was being. She thought about how she could try and turn things around. A weekly meeting was daunting, especially with the distance between them, but she knew it would help.

'I'd really appreciate that. And I know I need to make sure that I pay attention to the detail.'

'It's not a deficiency peculiar to you. One of the key skills every trainee learns over the course of the training years is attention to detail – I know it's a work in progress. That said, you need to make sure you're pushing that skill all the time. Check your work twice, three times. Swap with other trainees and ask for feedback if you have time. Things like formatting, consistency of defined terms are crucial! They're what mark us out as professionals. Yes, the law has to be right, but if it's hidden in something that looks like you've lifted it from some particularly rubbish website then clients lose faith.'

'I understand, I do.'

Nathan smiled.

'I'm sorry if I've been unapproachable. It probably won't change; it's no secret I can be short with people. Let's have the weekly chat and we can see if you feel a bit more comfortable. In return, do every piece of work to

SEAT 1: COMMERCIAL LITIGATION

the best of your ability given the time you have. Deal?'

'Deal. And thanks for all the advice.'

'We'll make a litigation lawyer of you yet.'

As they walked back, Alex realised that the tension was draining out of her. Much of the pressure, she thought, she'd put on herself. Nathan had been kind when she actually addressed the issues, although on his terms, and she knew he was right about her attention to detail. Most of all, she felt that she had entered fully into the professional world, sitting down with a senior colleague and addressing an issue of concern to both of them. As Carla said, when she mentioned the meeting at lunch, 'It's called 'training' for a reason. We're all learning and I think you've had this more difficult than most. I've never heard of anyone being told a mistake will be 'career limiting' before.'

Alex smiled.

'It'll get better from here. I can feel it.'

PART 2: DOING THE WORK

5 | CHEERFUL WORKING

When I was applying to university, my school organised a preparatory interview with the head of another, as part of its careers programme. The idea of this interview struck terror into me. Of course, that's precisely the reason to do it and I was strongly encouraged to participate. I turned up five minutes late with a knot in my stomach, slouched into the head's office, stared at the floor and answered the difficult questions very, very poorly.

In fairness to me, it was an odd and esoteric interview – the final question being something to do with halls of residence, a legal textbook and a light bulb, the point of which escapes me. The feedback to my headteacher was damning.

It had nothing to do with law, ability, or my career aspirations (or more accurately at that point, the lack of them). No, what the interviewer said they picked up in that hour and a half was my arrogance. The overwhelming disinterest I had in the process. My unwillingness to engage.

I was shocked. I'd been grateful for the opportunity and although the experience had been deeply unpleasant, that was because I thought I'd under-performed and was worried about it. Not the marker, I'd argue, of someone who didn't care.

My school kindly disregarded the feedback, and we all carried on, pretending it didn't happen. Still, it took several more positive interviews to exorcise the experience.

That interviewer was mistaken. Yet they had picked up something real, misinterpreting worry and background shyness for (misplaced) self-belief and (misguided) rudeness. It was a salutary lesson that life, including work, is all about impressions.

If I had the chance to be interviewed again, giving the same answers no matter how terrible, then good eye contact, enthusiasm and a warm tone (with a dollop of deference, given the situation) would have resulted in entirely different feedback. The substance was almost beside the point.

In this chapter we will look at how to approach work. There are two limbs to this: attitude towards the work and the various ways of doing it, and we will consider both. Bear in mind from the outset that the impression you give is an important part of your performance. You are a trainee and, while expectations are high, everyone understands there is much to learn. What your colleagues will want to be sure of is that you're doing your best work. In the spirit of 'show, don't tell' the best way to convey that effort is to make clear your commitment to the role. I call this visible effort and commitment, 'Cheerful Working'.

Attitude

So, what is 'Cheerful Working'? It's nothing more elaborate than this: in a high pressure services industry like law, working optimistically and cheerfully with your colleagues will be integral to your success. Perhaps this sounds naïve, platitudinal, but if you take the principle to heart it will make your career much more enjoyable.

That is not to say you should bottle up or conceal mistakes or serious worries. If you begin to feel the effects of stress at work for any reason, find someone you trust and talk about it at the earliest opportunity. What we're discussing here is a technique for packaging yourself and your way of working to your colleagues, presenting in the best possible light; it is absolutely not about putting on a front to your detriment, 'masking', or a method of concealing deep seated concerns.

Cheerful Working is simple in theory, more difficult to apply and even harder to maintain. In your relationships with your supervisor, your team, your peers, try always to be reasonable, helpful, and to contribute with a smile. When in stressful situations, take a breath. When you've been up for 36 hours to meet a particular deadline (it happens) maintain enthusiasm for the task at hand. That is a difficult thing to do, but it will be noticed.

This doesn't mean that you should feel put upon, compelled to accept

5 | CHEERFUL WORKING

any work that comes your way. Not at all. The point is to maintain control of your attitude and to start to regulate that most important thing, reputation, by being seen to be willing to help.

Inherent in any junior position is assessment. Senior colleagues will regularly consider whether you are capable of certain types of work. In theory, as your experience improves, so will the quality of your work and the level of trust will increase. Refusing to do work, being recalcitrant or even simply reluctant will count against you. Working cheerfully, you can have the best of both worlds: being seen as willing to challenge yourself and support the team by taking on the work while empowering yourself by setting parameters.

Imagine you have been asked to assist with a project. It's 10am and your supervisor wanders over, a coffee in hand. There's a research note that needs writing, together with a draft of a cover email to the client. Your supervisor will review before anything is sent out. You're busy already, with pre-existing work from your supervisor and others piling up, and part of you feels you won't be able to produce your best work. Should you take on the task — and, if so, how should you set about it?

It would be perfectly understandable for you to try to minimise your involvement and, perhaps, to feel hard done by if your supervisor insists. Managing these feelings is part of your training experience and you will find your own way to deal with competing demands (although you should always feel as though you can ask your supervisor or the head of the team for help or advice — see Chapter 8).

Yet, if you engage positively with the work there are likely to be benefits to you and the wider team. You will establish your reputation as a person willing to go above and beyond. Rather than letting down anyone who has already given you work, you can explain the situation and establish priorities — an important skill to learn. By being open and cheerful you manage your own emotional response so that you don't feel overworked or develop an immediate stress.

Rather than try to refuse or grudgingly accept, ready to cram the work in whenever you're able to find the time, take it cheerfully. Talk to the person giving you the work (in this case your supervisor) and explain:

You're very happy to do the piece of research and you can see how it would really help your development as it fits in nicely with another transaction you are currently working on.

You thought you'd mention that this other transaction is due to finish in the next couple of days and so your time is necessarily limited, particularly as there will be an all-day meeting to ensure everything is in order.

In addition, you're not entirely sure where to start looking for commentary on a particular aspect, so you'd welcome a ten-minute chat (at a time convenient to you both) to discuss where you might profitably concentrate your research efforts.

Still, you're really interested in the area, willing to help and you look forward to working on it together.

Ok, written down this looks excessively formal, and you will need to make it your own. The point I'm making is rather than trying to side-step work which you may end up saddled with in any event, show willing and take control. In a few short sentences you can communicate: (i) you are busy; (ii) you could do with some help to get you going with the work; and (iii) you're interested.

In short, smother people with kindness and where it is tricky to assist, don't emphasise the problems or limiting factors, but the desire to get involved.

Now, this may all sound a little passive aggressive. After all, what you're really saying is, 'I'll do my best to do this, but I'm busy, so don't hold your breath', and you will need to be very careful that this doesn't come across as a particular type of arrogance. There is always the risk that your seniors, busy people themselves, might see it in this light and simply ask you to get on with things! In my experience, a genuine application of the 'Cheerful Working' approach will operate in your favour, showing you understand that you are fully a member of the team and take your obligations to colleagues seriously, but equally that you are confident enough to stand your ground and ensure you are given the space and support you need to do a difficult job well.

It can be scary to make demands along these lines from senior people, and that's where Cheerful Working helps you: taking a positive, constructive and (buzzword alert) proactive approach is likely to prompt a similar response in turn. You are providing yourself with protection against a backlash and, at the same time, enhancing your 'would-work-with' factor.

This is all in a perfect world. In the real world, people may be critical if they think their work will suffer or not be picked up with the speed they'd like (however unreasonable that is), or you may feel you can't be cheerful and reasonable in every situation. Cheerful Working is a state to aspire to rather than one you *must* achieve or dwell in permanently. It is absolutely fine if you have moments where you simply cannot help other people because your workload is too great or where you feel in some state of conflict with a colleague – that will be true in any sort of work environment. The number of your colleagues that don't get along is probably higher than you think! But the more you channel that cheerful state the easier and more satisfying you will find your training years and, indeed, your future career.

Presentation

So, we've decided to accept the research note (in truth, there was little choice), but we've managed to communicate that we need to fit it around other commitments while remaining engaged – and, crucially, making *obvious* that willingness to engage. The next step is to actually do the research.

As we're talking in general terms, we're not interested in the legal content (and please note the discussion of AI in Chapter 14). Instead, we need to consider where to invest your time and attention to provide a professional piece of work to your supervisor.

During your initial professional legal training – whether via the LPC or the SQE – you will receive instruction on how to carry out and present research and the subsequent client advice. Yet it will be different when you are faced with this task in the context of a real world problem. At this point, other factors come into play beyond whether you have found the right answer: Is there a preferred way to present work? What tone should you take? How much detail is too much?

Your firm will have its house style. Remember, this is a template (or series of templates for different documents) which uses a set font, exemplar headings and a pre-determined numbering structure. In the alternative, it may take the form of a set of rules for production of any given document. Either way, house style provides a standardised approach to work produced by your firm. And that's important: in the same way that you recognise a brand in the wider world, perhaps even without noticing, in the legal world the firm is trying to establish and maintain its separate identity, its visibility. You will impress those you work with if you take the trouble to abide by these rules for presentation (and you should have been told all about it in your induction).

You have your template, you have carried out your research and written it up in draft. Next you need to make sure that the numbering is correct and that headings and titles are suitably distinguished. This may sound like a terrifically minor point. In fact, you may be confused that I've jumped over the important part – the substance of the research.

Well, first, I'm hoping that this book is being read by a cross-section of would-be solicitors, each of you looking at different areas of law. I can't cover them all; I wouldn't know where to start.

More importantly, it's the soft skills that I want you to think about. At school and at university the emphasis will have been on getting the correct answer; you won't be (overly) penalised for poor presentation in an essay, especially if you've written something brilliant (as we all hope to do). But remember that law is a business and legal advice (often written) is its product. If you bought a new television, opened the box and found the instructions printed in different fonts, with no consistency of headings and formatting, it would not only make it difficult to follow those instructions but would make you doubt the quality of the television. It would be undermined by association.

It's no different with legal advice. Of priority to lawyers (and to all

5 | CHEERFUL WORKING

those who provide professional services), is to provide assurance to the client that we have understood the issue at hand and that the advice provided is reliable. One of the fundamentals of giving that impression is to produce a document without mistakes, properly formatted.

'Proper' formatting will involve you ensuring it conforms to house style and that you have been consistent with your use of that style. You need to check that the font and size you have used for your text is the same throughout and, similarly, your headings and use of sub-sections follow a recognisable pattern. This is legal work and we can all – lawyers foremost! – agree it can be rather dry. But you are aiming to make this as readable, as user-friendly as you possibly can.

If your firm is a large one, you may have support, whether through a legal assistant or a document production team (by whatever name called). You don't have to be a master of Word to be able to get the formatting right, you can ask for help. However – and you may not believe me – it is something that almost all trainees neglect. You must pay attention; appearance counts for an awful lot.

Once you think you have the answer, you've written it up using house style and you've double checked for consistency and formatting, you're ready to move on to the cover email.

Cover emails are a regular trainee task. The idea is to draft an email to the client setting out the nature of the question to which you are responding, the answer you have found (in brief) and clarification that a more detailed summary of the issue is set out in the attachment (your piece of work). The email is the 'cover' under which the main advice is sent. Easy so far.

In any email you draft you need to be conscious of tone. Clearly when addressing anyone professionally you will take a very different approach to that adopted when emailing a friend or relative. But other than that, tone is a series of shades. Excessively formal and overly familiar emails will equally mark you out as new. With the aim of blending into the profession, give the email some thought. It should cover the necessary legal and commercial points, of course, but what else? It needs a suitable greeting, adopting the same form of address used by the addressee (so, if Sue Atkins has signed off as Sue, use Sue rather than Ms Atkins). It should be firm – you are providing advice – and written in plain English. Use paragraphs. Try to keep it concise.

Your approach will differ depending on the type of email you're sending and the circumstances. When you get to know a client well, your approach may become more casual (although that shouldn't impact on the advice given). Inviting a client to a dinner will make use of an entirely different tone to that used when giving legal advice. Emails to fellow lawyers may engender yet another approach. What I'm encouraging you to do is think carefully about what you write on *every* occasion – use the skills you have honed over your writing life and vary your output given the situation at hand.

'I liked this – thanks,' your supervisor says later that day, having reviewed your work. 'I think we can revisit the point about the directorship, but you've used house style and the structure of the note made it clear and readable. The cover email was good too – you mentioned the key issues and cross-referred to the memo, but what I particularly liked was the tone. The language was straightforward, generally encouraging, and to the point, and I liked the way you opened the email by noting that I had asked you to look into the point as a way to make an introduction.'

That is the response you're looking for, one you can achieve regardless of your legal ability and at any stage of your training.

The crucial take-away here, as throughout this book, is that this isn't an exam anymore – it's a new reality. Let your personality come through in your work; take a view on things. Part of the excitement of finally being out there and in a position to apply the theory you have learnt during the academic years is that you can now make practical suggestions about application of the law. It goes beyond simply finding what the law is. It's now about being creative, thinking deeply about a problem and applying your legal research skills to the issue at hand.

This is particularly so in the common law system: I once spent several hours on a call with a Spanish colleague who, after several determined

5 | CHEERFUL WORKING

days of research and ferocious thought, had concluded that under codified Spanish law, the answer was 'no'. They were very proud of this response, which was concise and firm and carefully thought through in the context of a rich legal tradition. Yet that is not how the common law works, it is much more free form, more able to provide an answer of 'yes' but requires greater parsing. That is now your role.

Showing some passion and personality will be the best way, without fail, to be noticed. Introduce some flair. And that doesn't mean colours and graphics. Instead, it's demonstrated in taking care over the work so that the result isn't something any other trainee could have lifted from a search of the appropriate database – it is recognisably yours.

This takes us back to going above and beyond: top and tail the underlying note with an executive summary and a conclusion; make it read as well as you can; and give a view – what do *you* think the answer might be given the commercial/employment/criminal context of the question being asked?

Doing the work

'Um, I didn't go to uni to sit here and photocopy.'

Ok, no-one's actually ever said that – at least I hope they haven't – but this apostasy nicely captures a couple of truths about being a trainee. The work you do will be balanced between the mundane and the challenging: inherent in a role where the work you receive is either too basic (or it's not cost effective) for more experienced people to do, and/or it's difficult by definition because it will be new to you.

That's good news – a challenge is what we want, it helps us grow into fully rounded professionals. Yet there will still be the business-as-usual work to do, and it will come in spades. That's also good news as you need to build your understanding on firm foundations and the best way to do that is to start with the basics.

Frankly, there's considerable mental relief in being asked to do some photocopying, preparing a bundle for the court (including pagination) or preparing a bible (the set of signed transaction documents which will be referred to in future as the definitive copy). If Alex experienced every day the stress of dealing with her career limiting matter, alone, in her first seat, then professional life would quickly degenerate into a series of disasters.

A few early pointers/reminders before we address the types of work available.

Remember we are approaching the work cheerfully. Nevertheless, and however much you take that to heart, you won't enjoy it all. In fact, there may be a particular seat you really can't stand (or understand). Don't let a bad (for whatever reason) experience make you question the whole project. The beauty of the multiple-seat system is that there is the time and opportunity for you to start again. Indeed, a seat you don't like may be helpful because it allows you, ultimately, to narrow down your choices to other areas for potential qualification.

Don't panic about not understanding the majority of what is being discussed around you. Legal practice has the common issue of 'too many TLAs' (three-letter acronyms, as the old joke goes). Why would you, for example, be able to follow any of the acronyms used by directors in a board meeting? These probably aren't legal terms in any event, rather terms specific to that business or its sector. Not following doesn't mean that you can't do the job, just that you are learning.

Ask questions. A critical one will be: how long should this take? Understanding the turnaround time expected gives insight into the depth of the task. In other words, if you are asked to do some research and the person giving you the work indicates they think it should take an hour, you know that they think the answer is relatively easy to find without recourse to specialist databases or trawling through files. It also suggests that they will be happy with a brief email setting out your answer rather than a detailed (and time consuming) memorandum.

This is something you need to play by ear. The answer may be more complicated than anticipated and/or take more time to find. An estimate of the time to spend on the task is just an indication of how complicated it is anticipated to be. It's not a guarantee.

As ever, it's impossible to provide a one-size-fits-all summary of trainee

5 | CHEERFUL WORKING

tasks. There are a wide range of law firms with differing cultures and approaches to training and an even greater spread of training providers. The experience of a trainee in-house will be vastly different to that of a trainee in a City firm: in-house teams tend to be much smaller and less segregated so that trainees may be much more involved in the business, perhaps even engaged in advising strategic decision-makers quite quickly. Contrary (often) to popular opinion, a trainee in a City firm may spend a lot more time photocopying.

The summary below reflects the likely standard jobs for trainees (to the extent there is such a thing), so that you can anticipate some of what might come your way.

Document management: The basic product of all lawyers (outside the courtroom) is the signed agreement. It doesn't matter what that agreement deals with: a divorce, a declaration of capacity, a commercial contract with a big multi-national, negotiating that document and arranging for its signature will be a key task. Dealing with the practicalities of signature is a typical trainee job – very often now done online via software – and preparation for signing may include everything from drafting ancillary documents (the common term for minor functional documents that support the main documents, such as board minutes), putting together a copy of each document used in a project and publishing the resulting pack (known as 'bibling', producing a 'bible'), to photocopying and bundling (normally in a litigation context).

In my world, as a corporate solicitor, a trainee would be asked to prepare the room for a completion meeting if one was to be held. This means being responsible for ensuring the final versions of each document are laid out ready for signing (not such an easy task, bearing in mind that negotiation often continues to the wire), setting them out in a sensible order (perhaps a cover sheet for each document, linking it to the number of that document on a master list), ensuring they are signed at the meeting, collecting them, taking certified copies, and sending the appropriate original documents out to the parties with a copy of the overall project, a bible. If, as is more common in the post-2020 world, everything happens virtually, then the same approach is required save for the documents will be agreed, shared, signed and managed online.

This is admin, yes, but highly skilled admin. Dealing with documents will become your life, but it is teaching you wider skills: organisation, understanding how to structure and manage a project, how to address clients and how to explain to them in simple terms what they are signing and why.

Research: If there is research to be done, it will be a trainee that does it (or at least starts it off). This could be one-off points of law, or more in-depth research for an article in a legal journal. It could be completely unrelated to law. It's possible to find out a lot about someone before you meet them and most clients/client representatives will have online professional biographies; research on attendees at upcoming meetings for senior team members might be a regular request.

Assist with training: An extension of the research role, it's common for trainees to be tasked with assisting at or in some cases leading training sessions for the wider team on new or evolving points of law. Presentations are part of life now: you will have plenty of time to prepare.

Drafting engagement letters: One of the first things the firm needs to do when it takes on a new client or starts acting on a new matter for an existing client is to put in place an engagement letter (sometimes known as a client care letter). This has two purposes. First, it sets out the scope of the work – what the solicitors will be doing/trying to achieve. This is often referred to as the 'scope of work' or 'scope' for short. Second, it sets out the terms on which the firm will act for the client for this specific project. There is all sorts of stock but important material set out in an engagement letter, including limits to the firm's liability, the named client contact (and their core team), dispute management procedures and so on. Fortunately, this is all in a standard form – so much so, you won't be able to depart from some of it without authorisation – and it is a typical trainee task to produce a first draft using the firm's template.

Advice to clients: This will vary from firm to firm and between departments. If you are training in-house then you will have a huge amount of 'client' contact from the get-go as you deal exclusively with the business of your employer (and its group of companies). If you're a trainee in a criminal law firm, again by way of example only, then you are likely to have your own files fairly quickly, responsible for your own clients/cases. There will undoubtedly be some client contact whatever your role, but in most cases it won't be front and centre in an advisory capacity. Nevertheless, you will be in constant contact with clients over practicalities: when a document will be delivered, where a meeting will be held and so on.

Taking notes and minutes of meetings/preparing file notes: *Always* assume you are required to take notes of any meeting you go to. These may end up being formalised into minutes of that meeting or they may just be notes for the file (a record for the future of what was said), but either way it's good practice to get into the habit of writing everything down. It's better to have some redundant notes than to be asked afterwards for a comprehensive 'who said what' and be unable to provide it.

Recruitment: Trainees are both the future of the firm and its current face. Closer in age to the students the firm wants (and needs) to recruit, you will almost certainly be asked to attend events at universities or local schools, talking about being a lawyer, your route into the profession including your experience of vacation schemes (and other routes, including apprenticeships) and tips for success. You will, of course, be able to mention how useful this book was in your preparations for joining the profession...

Given that training arrangements are agreed sometimes years in advance, most firms will make efforts to stay in regular contact with its incoming trainees and you will be called upon to attend events with those future stars to offer advice and encouragement.

Business development: Although there is no expectation for trainees to bring work into the firm, it is never too early to begin networking. It's an essential skill and one which is the subject of many other books. You will be asked to attend events with clients and there will be an expectation that you join in (within reason). Try not to shy away from these things or, on the other end of the spectrum, be too exuberant. Be yourself, enjoy yourself, speak normally (don't try and talk business) and people will warm to you. Local professional groups and law societies provide excellent opportunities to meet other junior people and to raise your profile in the profession and in your local area.

Billing/time management: Another task delegated to trainees is organising invoices to be sent to clients, critical in generating cash flow. Deciding what to bill is the responsibility of the relevant matter partner and producing a bill is the responsibility of the finance team (and due to very important legal accounting rules put in place by the SRA your firm will almost certainly have someone outside the legal team who is in charge of finance matters). You will be the conduit to get this invoice produced and, using diplomacy where necessary, delivered to the client.

Organising team socials: We will touch on this in more detail in Chapter 11 when we discuss options for getting involved in the life of the firm. In this context, I'm raising it more as a potential responsibility – rightly or wrongly it's often assumed that trainees have time to deal with what's frequently seen as peripheral activity and, again, rightly or wrongly, that they know good places to go! Socials are the life blood of a team, not some adjunct activity. If this comes your way, see it as an opportunity to make your mark on the team. Round up some other trainees to help and make it a night to remember.

Last, but unfortunately not least, helping out the partners: Pockets of law remain extremely hierarchical and there is still an element of 'what the partner needs the partner gets'. It's not unheard of to be asked to get coffee; to pop over to the car park across the way and bring round a car while your supervisor finishes a call; to be despatched to a restaurant to find a forgotten phone. It happens and will continue to whatever our private views about professionalism. Smile gracefully, help out and remind them of it at appraisal time.

5 | CHEERFUL WORKING

Passion, personality and proactivity

We've covered a lot of ground in this chapter, but we can capture its essence in three words: passion, personality and proactivity.

When it comes to doing the work, the best way to do it well and to enjoy doing it is to do it with passion – find a way to make it interesting to you.

Make your work stand out by giving your writing personality. A judiciously chosen layout. A sensible contribution to the debate. If you are inclined, use an elegant style or a rigidly legal one. Somehow, make it yours.

Impress those you work with by being proactive. The answers are (mostly) all there, in the paperwork, in the file, on a legal research website, at Companies House. Take that extra moment to think, 'How could I take this beyond the task I've been set?' One of the ubiquitous business phrases of the current age is 'added value' meaning, crudely, to go unexpectedly above and beyond what's anticipated. How might you deliver what you've been asked to while enhancing its utility?

You will see, I hope, that success as a trainee is not about natural legal ability or who you know. It's about enthusiasm and a critical eye, making the assignment, whatever it is, the best it can be.

Takeaways

» In your relationships with your supervisor, your team, your peers, try to be reasonable, helpful, and to contribute with a smile – this is Cheerful Working. This doesn't mean saying 'yes' to everything asked of you but rather demonstrating a willingness to help in some capacity most of the time.

» Always pay attention to presentation of your work. It is the firm's product and illustrates attention to detail. Use house style and maintain the brand. Proofread and check formatting. In any email you draft, be conscious of tone.

» Ask questions. Clarify the task and establish when a response is needed.

» Remember passion, personality and proactivity: find ways to make each task interesting to you, make it yours, think about how you can add value to your output.

6 | MANAGING MISTAKES

This chapter is about mistakes. You might think it's quite early to be talking about what could go wrong but if a single message came out of the research for this book, it was the desperate worry colleagues recalled from their training days about making mistakes.

Obviously, right?

In talking to trainees and the newly qualified about their concerns when starting their training and – for those further down the track – asking what advice they would give their younger selves, it was a repeating refrain that they (i) were most worried they would get something wrong; and (ii) would choose to dispel that concern as their chosen piece of reassurance.

Most people weren't pointing to a specific error (or potential error). The apprehension appeared to stem from fear of the unknown as much as self-doubt (hence the purpose of this book, to demystify the period of training). It's also notable that the chosen piece of advice was to allay that concern: to make the point that mistakes will happen and that it's not the end of the world when they do.

Convincing you of that is what this chapter seeks to achieve. You *will* get things wrong whether that's coming to a legal conclusion that's incorrect, filing the wrong document or simply picking up the wrong bits of paper from the printer. It's often not the mistake itself that causes problems, it's the reaction.

Once again, for the people at the back: mistakes will be made. Try to relax and do the best you can but know that they will come. It is, after all, a learning experience. Don't blow it out of proportion; the worst thing you can do is panic or to let worry hold you back. A highly experienced partner once told me, 'Anything can be solved with another piece of paper'.

This, of course, assumes you have told someone you suspect there's been an error and together you have worked out what that saviour piece of paper might look like. The good news is that you will always remember the answer – there's nothing like making an error to fix in the mind how it should have been done. If someone solves the problem for you, and you're confused about what went wrong, then make sure you ask.

First principles
First of all, and this is an important point, the mistake may not be yours. If you spot a problem, don't assume you're wrong. Don't dismiss anything that looks unusual to you or put it down to inexperience. To err is human and it may well be that someone else working on the file has missed a key issue. If you don't understand why something has been done in a particular way, if it is unclear to you, bring it up tactfully. You will either learn something (why it isn't the issue you thought it might be) or you will solve a problem or avoid a mistake (by spotting something no-one else has).

Tact is important: this isn't about point scoring, and it won't go down well if it looks as though you're trying to second guess decisions made elsewhere. Still, don't feel as though you need to accept material as gospel, particularly where it looks wrong to you. Use the point to start a conversation.

Next, don't have sleepless nights over an abstract 'what if?' A mistake is an inevitability that you make every effort to avoid; those efforts are doomed to failure! As we've said, the test of your mettle is not in keeping a perfect score sheet but in how you deal with mistakes that have been made. After some time has passed it will be a story to tell. Embrace the issue, correct it and learn.

Emails – Teams – Slack etc
Everyone from the top of the organisation downwards makes jokes via email or the internal messaging system (whatever your firm uses), and sometimes, when the number of people on the chain grows, whole afternoons can disappear to the wit of the local comic. As long as the work gets done, generally no-one will mind. That said, anything written down has

6 | MANAGING MISTAKES

the potential to spread, to go viral. The legal press is full of such tales of misadventure: for one example of many, at the time of finalising this book the lead headline on a major legal website was 'Bank solicitor who nicknamed colleagues 'Pol Pot', 'The idiot' and 'Jabba the Hutt' fined £15k.'

In the heat of the moment when you've crafted the perfect thing to say, a gem of a riposte, you will be tempted to put it down in writing despite it being just the wrong side of savoury. Pause for a moment and think how it would appear on the gossip pages of the legal press. And if it's still just that good…well, I'll leave that to your discretion. Never, ever, use the word 'banter'. It's basic common sense.

Let's return to legal mistakes. There is, of course, only so much you can do. If a disaster is brewing it may be you have no control over it, even if you see it coming.

A former trainee at a London firm tells a story about being asked to draft a lease break notice – a document terminating a lease part way through its term. The partner who initially assigned the work was subsequently pulled into a huge property portfolio reorganisation that became all-consuming and, despite the trainee's pleas, didn't find time to review the notice. The trainee, not understanding the importance of the notice, did nothing. The day before the deadline for service, the client realised the notice was outstanding and, as you might imagine, all hell broke loose.

This is the sort of situation you might find yourself in – although I hope you don't – and it can feel as though there's nothing you can do. The ball has, as the saying goes, already been dropped. The responsibility for the work lies with the partner involved, so in one sense the trainee in question discharged their responsibilities by doing the work and waiting for the lease to be reviewed. But professional life is about teamwork and being passive can easily lead to miscommunication and, ultimately, things being missed.

In a situation like this, I'd suggest being more demonstrative, sending repeat reminders. Send a message every day if you have to, even make a joke of it: 'Hi Andrew – sorry to bother you again, but it's my daily email about the break clause letter. Could you have a look at it as soon as you have a moment – or let me know who might be free to review? We told the client it would be with them to send out on Friday this week.' Pick up the phone or put a meeting in the diary. Better still, do all of them with the deadline in mind.

A call-back to proactivity

Being demonstrative, or resilient, or whatever we want to call it is linked closely to being proactive with your work, something we considered in the last chapter but it's worth revisiting.

It is tricky to get this right.

The easiest mistake to make is to try and complete the work as fast as you can and hand it back. A common misconception is that this evidences your talent and your enterprise – that you understand, for want of a better phrase, that time is money.

It doesn't. It will inevitably show that you can do a reasonable (although sometimes downright shoddy) job relatively fast: you're unlikely to have given yourself sufficient time to check the work closely. As with job applications, a couple of spelling mistakes, mixed font and anything hard to follow is likely to end up rejected and back on your desk. It's not that those small irritants mean you aren't a good lawyer – they just suggest you haven't paid attention to the detail, with implications for the quality of the legal work overall. And close attention to detail is *the* number one lesson for being a trainee.

A close second in terms of common mistakes is the temptation to 'gold-plate', agonisingly researching every point and writing a 20-page memo when a single page would have done. To some extent this comes with experience but, as we have discussed, understanding the time you have to do the work and its end use will give you an idea of what is appropriate. Done is better than perfect, so make it the best you can *given* the constraints you are working under and then discuss where you have got to with your supervisor or the person who gave you the work.

Third, and perhaps the worst of all worlds, is doing the work quickly and then sitting on it. This is a natural tendency: do the work while the

6 | MANAGING MISTAKES

instructions are fresh in your mind and you understand the task, save it somewhere in case you need to do some more to it, and wait to be asked.

Now, you will anticipate that your colleagues are busy; you will be busy. Waiting to be asked whether you have completed a piece of work can be hugely frustrating for the person who has given it to you. The answer when prompted of, 'Yeah, sure that's done: I did it a week ago', doesn't look efficient and on top of things, it begs the question: 'What were you waiting for?'

I understand the temptation, I really do. Letting go of work is hard – there might be errors, you may have missed something, there's a risk you have misunderstood the whole thing. That would be embarrassing. But the work could also be accurate and well produced. What it can't be is delayed. And this works in your favour – deadlines are your friends. Anything can be revised and reworked. This book is very different from the first draft and there are changes I would make to this final draft if I had more time. It is the very best it could be in the time that I had. At a certain point, one needs to finish a task and look for new ones. Don't frustrate the people you work with; do your best and then hand it over or, if needs be, ask for further guidance.

As we discussed earlier in this chapter, asking questions is important at the right time. The right time, however, won't be when you have thought about it for two weeks and finally get the opportunity to speak to someone who might know the answer – that's just two weeks of wasted time. If the task is complicated and you have follow-up questions, consider emailing them or put a time in the diary, prepare a list of those questions and run through them in one sitting. Don't sit and worry – no-one wants you to do that and it doesn't help solve the problem. Don't leave it a week before you look at the work (if you can possibly avoid it) and then realise you have lots of questions. Try and establish the parameters of what you're doing at the earliest possible point.

Remember, these are suggestions to help ease your way as a trainee. You won't always be able to adhere to them and you won't always need to. It's perfectly likely that asking rudimentary questions two weeks later won't bother anyone at all – they will help you without a word. Still, I trust you can see how this *could* irritate someone, especially under pressure. How it looks less organised, less professional. And that is the mindset I want you to have: how can I be most helpful, most thorough, in any given situation?

You are learning...

Don't forget that you are also new to the work and, perhaps, professional life. When you think something has gone wrong, don't panic, mention it to someone. You're not reinventing the wheel with the work you're doing; in the same way, almost anything that can go wrong already will have.

So, when you realise that an error has been made and, summoning courage, go and tell someone, sure that you're about to be sacked, you will inevitably be surprised by how calm your colleagues are and how reassuring they can be. Solving the problem, when viewed holistically, is good for your professional self-esteem.

How not to treat people

'A formal written warning? A FORMAL WRITTEN WARNING!?' And the legal PA bursts into tears. What could have prompted this?

Jamie is at fault. He's a trainee at a large firm. He's a year into his training and he has two seats under his belt. It hasn't been an easy ride – he's managed to irritate the PAs by (i) never saying hello in the morning; (ii) dropping work on their desks without acknowledgement; (iii) generally failing to see them as colleagues and to treat them as any sort of equal. Getting on the wrong side of the PAs is never a good idea.

The last 48 hours have been difficult for the whole team. A high-pressure transaction has just finished, with many people including Jamie and the partner he does most of his work for having been at work for over 24 hours. There's an air of celebration in the air, tempered only by a rather curt request from Jamie's boss to 'get his time down'. Jamie is well aware that he needs to record his time against the client/matter code. It's assumed that he's somewhat behind because of the recent intense workload. The matter partner is insistent because she wants to send an invoice to the client as soon as she can, taking advantage of the satisfaction (to all concerned) of a transaction well done.

Jamie, tired and looking forward to a well earned rest that evening, decides to head home. He does nothing about his time entries.

The next morning, Jamie arrives to be called into the partner's office. A member of HR is present and after some discussion, Jamie agrees that he hasn't recorded any time on this matter or, indeed, any other since he started the seat. He is aware of the daily time recording policy and offers little justification for his failure to comply with it. With much upset on both sides, Jamie is issued with a formal written warning.

Now this is extremely unlikely, but if Jamie has received prior warnings about time recording, then it's conceivable that a formal sanction could be applied. If such circumstances ever should arise, treat it as a learning experience. Perhaps you didn't understand how the system worked, or you struggled to find the best way to time record. There will always be a solution, in this case further training. Take the warning, discuss the matter honestly with the seniors involved and move on with good grace to progress your career. What you should not do is…

Jamie is irritated about the written warning. Asked to do a piece of administrative work that afternoon, he asks his PA to pick it up. Returning after lunch and asking for the work, Sue, his PA, tells him that she has prioritised something else as he hadn't said it was time critical.

Jamie sits down at his desk and copy types his written warning, changing the names, leaving it on Sue's desk. When Sue returns from a meeting and sees the warning, it looks sufficiently formal to alarm her, leading to the scene of recrimination where we started and the immediate involvement of senior people in the team and HR.

Impulsive actions like this will probably result in Jamie being asked to leave at the end of his training. He has no right whatsoever to try to bring a unilateral disciplinary action against his colleague!

Now, such an outlandish scene is extremely unlikely to materialise and, should it, would be symptomatic of a toxic culture at that firm and say very little about the individuals involved. The point I'm exaggerating to make is two-fold: Always treat people with respect. Never take your concerns out on others – own your errors.

Stress...and coping

Being a solicitor is hard. That's true of other professions and it's not a claim to uniqueness, but something you need to bear in mind. Acknowledging that pressure allows you to mollify the inner critic a little. It also means you can give yourself some perspective. It is a difficult job, prestigious precisely because of the level of difficulty, and what it requires of you is concentration and commitment. What it does not, or should not, require is constant fear of being wrong and the haunting shadow of work done in the day taking over every evening.

The profession is rife with stories about breakdowns, burnouts, leavers who couldn't take the pace. In reality, most firms take the welfare of their people extremely seriously; after all, the people are the product. Without the lawyers to do the work there is nothing to offer a paying client.

Still, it is demanding and there will be pressure to perform. So, it is important both to develop coping strategies and, if things get too much, to ask for help. Let's run through approaches to both.

Coping strategies will differ for all of you: one person's stress ball, is another's gym, is another's chocolate biscuit. Anything (within reason) that brings the blood pressure down in a tough situation is worth its weight in gold. Experience tells us that there are some simple ways which seem to help across the board:

- **Take a break.** The simplest thing to do is to get up from the desk and take a short walk. Whether that's to get a drink, some air, to talk to someone in another department or even just to go up and down in the lift a few times cursing the world for the direction life has taken you, the change of scene will make you feel better. Sometimes it can feel as though the work you are doing is the be-all-and-end-all – it isn't. Go outside, look at people walking around who don't know (or care)

about the board minutes you're drafting and you will regain perspective. The world is much bigger than our minuscule part.
- **Ask for help.** If you're struggling with something, don't wrestle with it in silent agony. Ask your supervisor, another trainee, someone with kind eyes in the department to discuss it with you. It's not cheating! It's a discussion between professionals about something that's puzzling – you will hear the partners doing that all the time. After all, no-one knows it all.
- **Structure the day.** Much professional anxiety comes from feeling out of control – you have too much work, not enough time, not enough help, you can't be sure of the answer. It's about insufficiency. The best way to combat this is to be organised and to know what you're going to try and accomplish each day. There will be (frequent) moments where your carefully timetabled day is thrown into disarray within the first five minutes as you're pulled onto a call or given some urgent and unexpected work to do. But if you have a clear idea at any given moment of the work you have to do and the time you have to do it, that will make you feel much more in control of the situation. Knowledge will take much of the tension away. It will also allow you to be clear about your capacity (see below). However you choose to plan your time, and whichever techniques you use, do more of it.
- **Be direct.** We looked at this in Chapter 5 when we considered strategies for saying no, and the same principles apply. If you're worried that you're too busy, say so. Put some time in your supervisor's diary and go through your work – a good supervisor will help you prioritise and strategise. They will (or should) defend you from too many overlapping demands. Crucially, they are much more informed about pipeline work than you; they know what's coming.
- **Get involved as much as you can in the life of the firm.** You might think, at first glance, that taking on extra activities could add to any pressure you're feeling, but actually the 'nail bed' principle kicks in. Spreading your responsibilities and interests over a wide area means the sting is taken out of each 'nail' of commitment. If the piece of

work in front of you is all you have to do, it can feel like a mountain to climb, but add to that an email about a work social event, a meeting of the firm's sustainability committee, a presentation to a local college about life as a solicitor, and, well, the psychological drama linked to that difficult piece of work is much reduced. There are simply too many other things to do for it to occupy you in the same way as it would if it stood alone!

- **Moan.** All employees do it and it will happen naturally in your cohort and teams. In my view, it's supremely healthy. 'Why do they NEVER give me warning about these calls?' 'Why do they INSIST on a meeting?' Complaining about the state of the working world has always been a secret pleasure of its inhabitants. Obviously, if this tips over into general team malaise, that's a problem – there's nothing more contagious than low morale. But managing that won't be your concern for a while. Moaning is a release valve for frustrations.

This advice presupposes that you're dealing with usual workplace niggles in a busy and frequently pressurised environment. 'Coping' implies ways to lessen or disperse that pressure – to breathe a bit more easily. However, should you start to feel severely unhappy or anxious, it is very important that you speak to your supervisor, HR or a medical professional. Or, indeed, anyone you trust. As soon as possible. All firms have access to occupational health and there are now several charities whose sole focus is the mental health and wellbeing of lawyers.

I hope it doesn't need to be said, but there is absolutely no shame in asking for help. That is the bravest and hardest thing to do and, despite a rather brusque front, the legal profession in general is very responsive to any request for help. I doubt the firms would put it in these terms but they work their people hard and they work them long – they know that sometimes people will begin to struggle and they are prepared to deal kindly and generously in those situations.

Two things I can't emphasise enough: (i) there is no rhyme or reason to that struggle being triggered – it is no reflection on the talent or aptitude of the individual; (ii) it has no impact on your future career which will continue to be as varied and stellar as you have the energy and desire to make it. The earlier you speak to someone, the earlier you can start to change your working patterns in ways that suit you.

Takeaways

» It is a truth universally acknowledged (to borrow from a far superior writer) that trainees going into the profession are worried they will get something wrong. Mistakes will happen; it is not the end of the world. Those who have experienced training want you to know this.

» If you spot a problem, don't assume you are wrong. Ask questions at the right time. If you realise that *you* have made an error, always tell someone. A problem shared is a problem halved.

» Avoid 'banter'. There is nothing wrong with enjoying a joke with colleagues, but side-step anything that you would blush to see reported in the legal press (or, indeed, anywhere else).

» Be proactive. Follow up with those who have given you work, don't sit on material when you have completed it, and remember that you are learning so be kind to yourself.

» Identify and use the coping strategies that work for you, including taking regular breaks and planning your day. Should you start to feel severely unhappy or anxious, it is very important you speak to someone you trust.

7 | MANAGING TIME

There are two sides to any discussion of managing time. The first is practical: almost all law firms record time against a project (or 'matter') number, and it's that cumulative time, across all the participants in a project, which provides the starting point for invoicing. The second, and more interesting aspect, is how *you* manage your time. It may be a shock to the system how much you are left to your own devices to balance your work in a way that suits you. You may be asked to complete a piece of work in an hour, a day, a week, but that's about all that will be said. It will be for you to organise your activity, taking into account other obligations – other pieces of work, other contributions to the firm (see Chapter 11) and, most importantly, your life away from law.

Time recording

Let's deal with time recording first. For those of you familiar with the concept, you may want to skip ahead, although you will find it useful to understand the idiosyncrasies in a law firm context. Despite the emergence of fixed and capped fee services (see later in this chapter for a more detailed explanation of these terms), law firms still manage themselves by tracking the time of their employees. In addition to being the basis for generating fees, time recording allows firms to monitor the amount of time spent on each matter (and therefore where to pitch future quotations so that the firm makes money) and to set and review targets for individuals – including trainees.

People new to law often struggle with the idea of accounting for every minute (or, more accurately, six minutes) of the day. Firms – and individuals – approach it differently. Many firms use app-based solutions where you have the facility to trigger a timer whenever you work on a particular

BEING A TRAINEE SOLICITOR

file. This can then be imported to the central time recording system, saving some time. Some individuals – the luddites among us – keep a written log of what they have worked on during the day and then submit the readings in one go at the end of that day. Others complete a time entry directly into the system at the end of each piece of work. There are any number of ways to do it – but it must be done!

This may sound easy – even fondly 'retro' given the state of current technology – but failing to keep up-to-date with time entries can quickly mean it becomes impossible for you to rectify the situation. Let's unpack this a little and go through the basics.

The principle is simple: every minute of every lawyer's day is recorded via six-minute increments. To do this, lawyers enter details of what they've been doing throughout the day into software designed for the purpose. It can be slightly unwieldy – I'm sure you will hear stories at your respective firms – but whichever programme your firm uses the requirements will be the same: (i) a record of the time spent against (ii) a number or code, known as a client/matter number, together with (iii) a description of the work that has been carried out, known as the 'narrative'. An example of a client/matter number might be 999999.00000, where the numbers before the full stop identify the client and the numbers after identify the project (or matter) that is being worked on.

Some clients only ever bring one project (an owner of a business who is selling up and retiring); regular clients may have many different projects that are being worked on simultaneously by lots of lawyers across the firm. All will have a number. The idea is to capture all tasks carried out during the day and so there will also be numbers, in similar format, for every activity; this will include internal training, research, pro bono work, and even social events.

Now, as a matter of convention the minimum time for each task is six minutes – this is the base unit for recording time. In other words, to the extent you spend less than six minutes on a matter, you record six minutes (or one unit of time). Should you spend 24 minutes on a matter, perfect as it's a multiple of six – you record 24 minutes or four units of time. If you spend 25 minutes on something, it would be rounded up to 30 minutes or five units of time. This may seem a little strange, but clearly accounting for each minute would be an administrative nightmare, not worth the effort. You might say that five minutes is the smallest amount of time anyone could reasonably spend on a professional task, but the six-minute unit is much easier to use when billing by the 60-minute hour. So that is what law firms do (along with many other professional services companies including accountants, auditors, many consultants and so on).

As you might have experienced when trying to keep a diary up-to-date or in sticking with an exercise regime, habit is everything. If you get behind with your time entries it is very difficult – and extremely boring – to try and recreate them. The ideal is to complete them at least every day. Your firm is likely to have a policy requiring you to take a certain approach to time entries, so make sure that you follow those requirements (again, this will be explained to you when you join). This might well require, say, that all time is recorded within a certain number of days (which, certainly in larger firms, is tracked); should it not be, there will be an impact on salary and the possibility of promotion. That aside, the simplest way for you to keep your sanity is to record your work as you go.

How do you do this?

Keep a notebook on your desk (or do it via OneNote or the app used by your firm if there is one) and jot down each thing you do. 'Phone call – Bob O'Brien – Jane Pharmaceuticals – discussed the non-executive director appointment letters – 10-10.15.' You can then transfer this to the time recording system at the end of the day. If easier, do it on your phone. As I say, your firm's time recording software is likely to have a similar function.

Insert the comment directly into the time recording system as you complete each piece of work. As I mentioned, if your firm has software which allows you to set electronic timers, that can be a huge time saving because you can set them with client details, drag and drop into the system and then reuse when you want to do further work on the same matter. You need to be the sort of person who remembers to click these smart timers

BEING A TRAINEE SOLICITOR

on and off, otherwise you won't have accurate recordings. I am not one of those people – I'm too easily distracted. Find what works for you.

It won't be generally advised, but if you don't keep a record of work as you go, you can review emails sent and received at the end of each day and work out the approximate time you spent on each task. This more casual approach relies on you updating your time entries at least daily – if you leave it longer, you won't be able to remember what you've done and your time entries won't be accurate.

Why is it important that the firm has accurate and timely time entries from its lawyers?

First, from your perspective: you will have targets involving both your fee earning i.e. the hours worked on client matters, and your contribution to the firm i.e. training, CSR and any other volunteering work. If you don't get into the habit of recording your time regularly, the result will be an underestimation rather than an overestimation of that time. In the absence of a record, most people (especially junior lawyers) will err on the side of caution: a 40-minute call becomes half an hour; 24 minutes spent on a letter becomes 18 minutes. This means that it is harder for you to reach your targets, if you have them.

In addition, you have an obligation to your client and your employer to make sure that you accurately reflect the time you have spent on a piece of work – it is part of your duty of care to your client and your contractual obligation to your employer. In the litigation context, it will be important in terms of cost estimates where submissions are being made to the court. Keeping your time recording up-to-date means it will keep your seniors and clients happy, and you won't receive the increasingly terse emails telling you to up your game.

From the firm's perspective, ensuring that individuals keep their time up-to-date is critical. The system will allow the partner who is responsible for any given matter to see at a glance how much time has been spent on it. For large projects with many people working on them across different departments, time reports will be the only way to keep clients advised of costs. Clearly, if time has not been recorded or closed (meaning entered as final on the system rather than in draft – we'll come back to this shortly) then there is no way for the partner or the client to understand what costs are being incurred. And on a large project, these costs will be accruing substantially from day to day.

In a similar manner, the firm's management uses time entries to test the capacity of each team. There is a notional (and finite) amount of work that can be done if every person is completing client work in line with their targeted (expected) hours. If, overall, the team is working at 70% of that figure then more work can – and must – be taken on. If those figures are incorrect, then the team runs the risk of being overworked and stretched. The principle remains true whatever the size of firm; every firm needs to keep an eye on resource.

In short, it is in everyone's interests to ensure that time keeping is up-to-date. Few people enjoy it, but it is necessary and the way the business operates.

You will hear people talking about 'closing time' – a metaphysical expression with the rather prosaic meaning of submitting your time entries as final. I mentioned it above. Whichever system you're using, the entries you submit initially sit on the system in draft, amendable, form. Perhaps you think you might do more work on that matter later that day or you aren't sure that you have the summary of what you did quite right; whatever the reason, until submitted this time recording won't show up more widely. You must remember to submit regularly. It can lead to considerable irritation on all sides if, when a project is complete and invoiced and has been over for some time, overdue time entries are then posted to the system. That time cost will need to be written off. It may also have target or promotion implications for those latecomers, as mentioned above.

You might think I've spent too long on a simple technicality (and well done for sticking with this chapter so far). As I've said many times already, the idea of this book is that it helps you to prepare for the reality of practice. Time recording – while not a difficult concept – is something that takes getting used to. Giving you some context and explaining how your time recording has wider significance than simply an administrative task with some vague connection to billing, helps in understanding its importance.

Let's consider some more specific ways in which you can make time recording easier for yourself and others.

When you are given work, always ask for the client/matter number. It may be that the number is still being set up as the various internal onboarding procedures are complied with (see Chapter 2), but ask the question as you will need it as soon as it becomes available.

Record all your time. This is a mantra you will hear often from seniors. Don't reduce the time you put on the file because you think it took you 'too long'. For trainees especially there is a temptation to write down the time they think *should have been* spent on a piece of work rather than the actual time spent. Yet again, there's no such thing as a 'correct' time entry. The work takes as long as it takes: it may have taken you longer than someone with more experience; it may have taken you longer because it was difficult; it might have taken exactly the average amount of time (were this to be calculable). The point is that you are not in a position to judge. Don't sell yourself or the firm short by underestimating or deliberately cutting down your time. This is especially true if you're entering time after the event and there is some element of estimation.

You may find that certain senior people in your firm get very concerned about the amount of time you are recording. This is because where there is a significant disconnect between the amount it is possible to invoice and the amount of time recorded on a matter, there is likely to be some internal explaining for the matter partner to do. Ignore such concerns.

It is for the partner to determine what is ultimately invoiced (it is, after all, their business). As we have already seen, it is also important for management purposes to understand how much (notionally) projects cost to run and the level of utilisation (your time) they require. You should always accurately record your time, and the vast majority of partners – and all sensible ones – will support you in this. Be scrupulous.

Write sensible summaries of the work you have done. As we saw earlier on, this is known as 'narrative' and is designed both for internal and external use. Internally, it allows whoever is approving the invoice for a client to look through the work done and determine if certain time should not be included. For example, you might be brand new to a department and spend two hours working out how to access a particular database that is regularly used in that field. You would properly record this time against the matter you were working on, but in most cases anyone reviewing a draft invoice would delete this time from the total – it's really training time for you and therefore an overhead of the firm.

Externally, clients often request a copy of the time break-down and accompanying narrative be included with the invoice – after all, they want to see what they are paying for. Remember this and make sure that your write up fully reflects the work you are doing. Rather than 'Lease review', which reveals very little, aim instead for 'Review of lease for X address; written report (X pages) for the attention of X (name of client contact)'. There may be further detail that you consider appropriate. It should go without saying but given the potential for time entries to go to clients they must at the very least be spell-checked and, if you want to keep things interesting, be written with a little lyrical flair.

Similarly, try not to use too much jargon. It's tempting to lapse into shorthand, especially after a long day when filling in your time entries is something to get done as quickly as possible. However, it may be that the person raising the invoice is in another department and doesn't understand the work you have been doing (beware acronyms in particular) or, worse, it goes to the client unamended and simply comes back with a request for clarification. Plain English is always best and will lead you towards writing something more descriptive and therefore useful, in line with the advice immediately above.

Remember that there is a link between capacity and your time records. As you will recall, capacity is jargon for the time you have available to take on new work: 'Do you have capacity for this?' will become a familiar refrain. If you accurately record your time on a regular basis then it will help you to answer that question honestly. It is no help to you or your colleagues if you take on work you don't have time to do or if you don't agree to do work because you aren't sure how much time you will have. Both of these concerns can be addressed by close attention to your work log: What did a similar piece of work require in terms of documents? How long did it take you last time? If you are recording more than your target hours, do you have capacity for more? (Probably not.) As an aside, there is no need to panic if you don't fill your day with client-related work. For the rest of the time you are likely to be doing administration or non-client work. As ever, there will be a number.

Just so you're aware, there is a divergence of opinion about whether or not all internal discussions relating to a client should be recorded against that client's number. My view is that they should be: if it is client-related work then record it but be specific. Who were you talking to, by name, and what was the discussion about? If it was just research or thinking time, what were you pondering? What were the outcomes/actions? If you feel it is appropriate, there is usually space for a purely internal comment to the person responsible for raising the invoice and you could mark a particular entry for future attention, querying whether that time is appropriate for billing. Once again, this won't be a decision for you – you're simply raising the point.

As an overall comment, try not to regard time recording as an administrative exercise that bores you. Instead, see it as a matter of satisfaction. Unlike in many other jobs you have a record of precisely what tasks you have carried out and which projects you have been involved in. It is your link to the firm's profit-making potential; the reason you are paid. See it as evidence of your participation in the firm. Be creative – don't just put anything that isn't client work on a general admin number, but use the record to demonstrate the different facets of your participation: there will be management codes, social codes, volunteering codes, knowledge contribution codes. Use them, and when it comes to appraisal time (much more frequent for trainees who have them at least every six months, often every three if your firm asks for mid-seat appraisals), you will be able to separate out these sub-categories and use them to frame the discussion.

7 | MANAGING TIME

Effective time management

We have discussed the empirical nature of entering your time. Now let's consider how you might go about managing your time effectively, so that those time entries reflect your ability to work efficiently. Before we go forward, I should note that this chapter isn't designed to increase your productivity. Many other titles and techniques are available which do so and help you to plan your day to your advantage. Instead, the rest of this chapter explores the tools you will have at your disposal to assist you in your work.

Let's start with the practical – use your resources. If you have access to a PA, they will know all the firm's systems extremely well and, even better, they will have contacts across the firm. If there is anything you need that they can't solve, they will know someone who can. If you are fortunate enough to have external administrative resources, use those too. For example, some firms purchase outsourced services to provide round the clock support, such as dictation, document production and design work, often in other jurisdictions. AI products will of course assist with these kinds of tasks, but there's nothing quite like human review.

A common – though entirely understandable – approach taken by many trainees, especially in their first year, is to try and do too much themselves. Your task is to understand the legal and commercial reality you find yourself in; yet you will find, late at night, the thing that brings you to the verge of tears will be document formatting. Wherever possible, pass that sort of work on to those with specialist skills. Additionally, try techniques that may be unfamiliar to you. Dictation, for example, is still very common in law firms and can be a fantastically flexible way to get ahead with your work.

Many people find dictation tricky to begin with, probably because speaking your thoughts requires that you have a direction in mind and some ability to formulate your research memo or email in your head, remembering what you have said *and* what remains to be said. It can be very different from sending a voice note or dictating to WhatsApp. It's not to everyone's taste, but it can be an astonishing time saver.

BEING A TRAINEE SOLICITOR

Imagine walking home from the train station and rattling off two or three letters for processing overnight. (Although I can't emphasise this enough: this must not include confidential information such as client names. The legal press can give you examples of lawyers who have worked on material on the train where someone looking over their shoulder has read the work and disclosed it.) After the 10-minute walk home you upload the files to a central system (or submit via the app – it will depend on your firm) and request it for 9am the following morning. You could, of course, dictate straight into a phone and voice recognition software will write your content as you speak. Clearly that won't give you the letter formatted in house style that we are looking for here – hence the use of the system offered by your firm.

Lo and behold, when you arrive at work the following morning, three letters await. You will need to proofread them, and it is very likely you will need to make substantial adjustments, but the documents exist and are ready for your editing. And this isn't something purely for the larger firms; reasonable pricing from outsourced service providers means that there are more options than ever for this kind of support and many firms are taking advantage.

I've concentrated on dictation here because it remains underused professionally, odd given that the new generation to the workforce is very comfortable dictating to a phone. The point is wider: explore ways of working that help you. You could handwrite emails or time entry narratives and ask your PA to type them up ready for you to check, cut and paste. You could keep a file of emails sent to you by other people which include terminology or ways of putting things that you like and can recycle at a later date – there are gems to be found everywhere. Give some thought to how you can make your life easier. Training is hard enough without adding to the challenge by starting every piece of work staring at a blank screen (and see below and Chapter 14 on the assistance offered by AI). Investigate ways to get you going.

Time saving techniques will help you, but you will frequently have competing deadlines often set by different people. How do you deal with this?

7 | MANAGING TIME

Start a list. It can't be overstated how useful a 'to do' list can be. Write down all the tasks you want or need to finish that day, however minor. This provides a clear line of sight to the end and tasks can be ordered appropriately. This list will be whole for about five minutes – almost immediately you will be given more work or told something has fallen away. And you won't get through everything however hard you try. Like shovelling sand, there will always be more, so see your list as a way to create some structure out of chaos, not the tasks of Hercules that you must complete before you're permitted to see the sun again.

Triage. Now you have your list, it's time to organise it. What are you going to prioritise and why? You're probably familiar with the term 'triage' from medical dramas – a way of assigning gradations of seriousness to patient injuries. In a less dramatic way, we can use the same idea to think about work. Which of the tasks is critical, either because of its timetable or its importance? Which are urgent, but have some flexibility in terms of delivery or perhaps you have already broken the back of it? Which are non-urgent – ongoing or housekeeping tasks? Once you've broken the tasks down, you have a good idea how your day will look. It might not be the case that you immediately begin the crucial tasks. Sometimes doing something simple, writing a short letter saying that a hard copy document is enclosed, or sending an email saying you can assist with a file, can be a helpful way to get the work juices flowing. The important thing is to give some attention to the *process* of organising the work, rather than randomly picking up jobs and moving between them.

Having a plan also allows you to explain to others in your team how you intend to spend your time. Should a senior associate summon you on to a conference call when you're really busy, being able to explain why you will struggle to attend because you have particular jobs to get done is much more likely to find a sympathetic ear than a protestation that you have a lot on without being able to explain quite what.

Communicate. As we have discussed elsewhere, you must always ask when work needs to be delivered. So, when you come to organise your time, you will have certain deadlines in mind. Never be afraid to discuss the status of your work with colleagues, no matter how senior. You may find you receive varying responses – it is a fact of the working world that one answer might be simply to get on with it – but most people would rather discuss timing of delivery than find the work is missing when they expected it. In a busy department, don't assume that people know what work you have on your desk and the associated deadlines. Your supervisor will have a rough idea, but no-one else will. It's ok to raise the issue and it might be the case that certain things you thought were urgent are no longer, and you can amend your list appropriately.

Organise your emails. You will be expected to file all matter-related emails in a folder which can be accessed by all the people who are working on that project. It's also worth keeping your own files. These tend to take the form of mirror files of each project so that you can continue to easily review work you have done, or they can be much more general – example documents, an email you thought was worded well, a useful link. Whatever and however you think best to organise it, if you can find your way around it works. At busy times you may receive hundreds of emails a day, and going back and filing after the event or searching for something you know you've done once before but can't quite remember when will be a real ordeal. Try to file in a manner helpful to you and at least on a daily basis.

Use generative artificial intelligence but be cautious. We will discuss AI in more detail in Chapter 14 when we look at the future of training. It is a powerful tool with immense potential to help you with all sorts of typical trainee tasks – research, first drafts of emails, client research. It can save you time and energy. However, you must be clear about how you are using it. Your firm will have rules around the AI that can be used and the tasks it can be used for. It's acknowledged to be unreliable and the output will always need careful review. Don't get me wrong, it is already a mainstay of practice and you will need (and want) to use it. It simply needs to be used within the parameters your firm has put in place.

Reflect on what you have achieved. One former trainee told me they created a 'good news' folder, where they saved emails with compliments on work well done. This was for their eyes only but gave a welcome boost whenever something wasn't going so well. No-one will accuse you of arrogance if you do this (indeed, no-one need know). It's a great way of providing evidence to yourself that you are producing good work and that you're learning and improving. This can also be a boon at appraisal time, especially if the comments are from clients. There is nothing wrong with promoting yourself and recording your successes; that is part of the role of an annual review.

A similar but more introspective resource is a reflection journal: a record of how you feel about the work you're doing. People can be very suspicious of this idea, but it's actually a great way of tracking your improvement and growing confidence. A reflection journal provides a space for honesty about your reaction to the whole experience of traineeship, to individual pieces of work, to your successes and your failures. You will be surprised how much confidence can come from looking back at those initial thoughts two or three seats later and realising how far you've come and how much you have learnt.

What could a reflection journal contain? It's intended as a safe space to note down not only frustrations and failures, things to learn from, but also successes – 'today is a good day because…' should be a well used phrase. You might structure it as a series of bullet points, things you need to remember: 'Always check for Companies House fees'; 'Mo likes a hard copy.' If you find it useful, it can be more elaborate, explaining why you enjoyed a piece of work, why it went well – both technically and why it dovetailed with your way of working or personality. It is easy to overestimate how much of a seat you will remember when it comes to qualification. You will have a record of the work you have done, in whatever guise your firm requires and in your required time recording, yet something more intimate and personal will help you when the time comes to make up your mind, filling in the missing part: how you felt about what you did.

As I say, journals aren't to everyone's taste, but I encourage you to try it in quiet moments. If you take to it, it can be an invaluable learning tool, providing a sense of self-assessment and growth that you can't really achieve via any other form of appraisal.

Finally, consider others. We talked earlier in this section about triaging in the context of your emails. Similarly, if your work involves someone else in any capacity, whether someone else in your team or in another department, the more notice you can give them that you will need their assistance, the better. Think ahead and send instructions as soon as you can. You are likely to earn goodwill that way.

Handovers

As you move from one seat to another, your key task will be to hand your ongoing work to the incoming trainee. It works in your favour to make this as seamless as possible. It helps limit the plaintive follow up calls asking for further information as you try and settle into your new location, and it also makes you look good with the department you've just left. This is important if you have thoughts of returning there (or even if you simply want to keep your options open).

Despite being a fact of trainee life, it's unlikely that you'll get much guidance on how to deal effectively with handovers: it's very much left to your discretion. As you'll need to do this at least four times during your trainee experience, it's worth us considering what the optimal handover looks like.

The best handovers will take place in two stages – a written note and a follow up call or meeting. Have the call after the seat change as it allows your replacement to read the note, get the lie of the land and prepare any questions they may have. The note, then, will be the main driver of a good handover – your talking point and pretty much the sole source of information for the 'new you'. Be alive to who will be replacing you. An incoming fourth seater may need less information than someone just joining the firm.

Handover notes can get out of hand very quickly. You might have 20 or 30 matters that are worth mentioning and trying to incorporate sufficient detail for someone to move forward with each of those matters independently can quickly end up with pages and pages of text. Hard to follow and almost useless. So, what are you trying to achieve and why?

The simple answer: a smooth transition. To condense all the (pertinent) knowledge in your head (who to deal with at the client; the outstanding points for negotiation; long-term objectives; short-term necessities), into a static document. A document that someone can pick up and, accounting for the inevitable fog that surrounds trying to understand and run with a job half done, take from it all key information. This means it needs to be concise but complete; forward looking but with necessary context. It is not an easy task!

And why go to all this trouble? It demonstrates your professionalism. It is in the firm's favour – clients can get very concerned about changes to a team working on their material, despite the trainee change over being a regular occurrence. An efficient handover will be remembered by the team. Here's a rough structure you could use as starting point.

- State the project name (if any), together with the parties, the names of representatives (i.e. the key client contact, legal representatives) and their contact details.
- Then give a short summary (three sentences maximum) of the matter before listing the major outstanding issues in bullet points.
- Follow this with a list, again in bullet point form, of the immediate next steps i.e. those things your replacement needs to pick up and do quite quickly (try to limit to three or four actions).
- Provide a list of the major documents, their location(s) or reference(s) – the place where the documents are stored on the firm's document management system or similar.
- Finally, provide notes or any general comments you think are necessary to contextualise the above.

This is only an illustration. Nevertheless, this summary gives you the tools to start to think carefully about how you would organise a handover; the more creative and innovative you can be the better. Amend in any way you like and if your firm has a particular way of doing this, take care to abide by those rules (with any improvements this section might have suggested to you).

As you leave the seat, it is tempting to cut and run. However diligent, there is part of all of us that, when faced with a new challenge and a change of pace, looks forward rather than back. The handover isn't just admin – a final burden you could do without – but rather an opportunity to tie up loose ends and to extricate yourself from the department on your terms. Leave your mark and do it right.

If you are the incoming trainee, make sure that you read the note in advance of the meeting or call to discuss it. Write down questions – things that you can't follow from the note, thoughts on next steps, anything that might be of interest to you. My top tip would be to ask about personalities, both at the client and in the new department. It's sensible not to write these things down – no-one wants an inadvertent character assassination left on the printer – but there's no harm in discussing it with your trainee colleague. Personality plays a big role in law firms: partners and seniors at the top of the tree have a huge influence on the behaviour and culture of a department. Clients, similarly, will have reputations that proceed them. Ok, it's limited information but it's worth knowing. You can use it to prepare for the first conversations and anticipate how someone might react to you as a newcomer.

Appraisals

Appraisals have already been mentioned in this book as a time to raise issues and successes. They are important. An appraisal is a formal, ring-fenced opportunity to sit down with your supervisor, one to one, and discuss frankly how things are going. It can be unnerving, but it will always be useful.

There is a five-step approach to dealing with appraisals:

(1) **Dedicate time.** Make sure the time is blocked out in your diary and your supervisor's. Try not to do it on the fly, although a trip to a coffee shop is fine. You don't want to be interrupted or rushed.

(2) **Reflect in advance.** Give some thought in advance of the appraisal to what you've enjoyed, areas where you would like more experience, particular feedback you think might help you. It's not a one-way street – you'll get more out of the exchange if you actively participate rather than passively letting your supervisor lead.

(3) **Do the paperwork.** As ever, take some notes as there is bound to be a form to fill in, either before the appraisal to be revised in light of it, or after the event. Either way, it's easier to write as you go rather than try and make it up at the end of the process. The forms are important because they are the standing record of your progress. They won't determine anything, necessarily, but if you find a department you love and your supervisor or main contact leaves, it will be the written appraisal form the team looks back on should you apply for a job. The forms should read as well as you can make them. Treat it as a chance to demonstrate your written communication skills.

(4) **Agree goals.** Set and agree some outcomes/next steps from your discussions. The goals should stretch you and it's an opportunity to say if you have an area of interest that you haven't yet been able to explore. If the goals can be designed to benefit the wider team, that will always help to keep you in the collective mind: carrying out a research project and giving a presentation to the department or beginning a newsletter. Be creative and ambitious.

(5) **Ask questions.** This is a key learning opportunity, so ask for feedback from as many people as you can, not only on work done but on your general approach. This is your chance to find out how someone established in the profession is responding to the way you work. In the future, when you are qualified and running your own projects or cases, the judgements and responses of opposing lawyers to your way of practice will be the determining factor (in most cases) in its smooth running. Getting honest feedback on your approach to colleagues is as important as how you have dealt with the complexities of the law. No one will be brutal unless, frankly, you are not cut out for the profession, and I suspect that will become obvious – not least to you – at a much earlier point!

An appraisal can be intimidating. It can also be seen, on occasion, as a waste of time. It should be neither of those things. It is a time to discuss what's going well, not so well and to establish aims and goals for the rest of the seat. Nothing should come as a surprise, particularly if your communication with your supervisor has been regular and clear (see Chapter 8). It is a chance to really explore your performance and the opportunities that might be open to you. Grab that chance with both hands.

Takeaways

» Time recording – accounting for each six-minute increment of each day and what you have done with it – is fundamental to law as a business. There are many different approaches to time recording and your firm will have tools to assist you. However it works for your firm, keep time entries up-to-date: it's how fees are generated and impacts on performance reviews!

» Use the resources available to you. Don't try and do it all yourself.

» When you change seats, think of the incoming trainee and arrange a practical, action-focused handover based on a well-balanced note.

» Consider a 'good news' folder for compliments on work well done. It's a great way of providing evidence to yourself (and others) that you're producing good work and that you're learning and improving. This is also a boon at appraisal time.

» Remember the five-step approach to dealing with appraisals: dedicate time, reflect in advance, do the paperwork, agree goals and ask questions.

SEAT 2: PLANNING

'OF FROGS'

In which Alex changes department, finds herself the only trainee, discovers how to reconcile a bypass with an endangered frog and (sort of) makes the national press.

'Ok so we're agreed.' A pause. 'We put a female frog in the big cage and leave it there with plenty of food and water. The males take the tunnel under the motorway to get to the female and the others follow. The road goes ahead, upkeep of the tunnel is with environmental, replacement of Miss Frog takes place every other day and we're all happy. That where we are?'

Alex blinked, taking it in. Is this really where they had ended up? A whole day of discussion and frog preservation had come down to the birds and the bees.

A woman at the end of the room swallowed, cleared her throat and made to speak. Didn't. Sat back in her chair, moved forward again, colouring slightly. Alex had marked her down as 'Frog Lady' in the minutes she was taking – the card she'd been given described her, more diplomatically, as the Environmental Planning Liaison Officer. Alex could tell, by the fidgeting, this was not going to be good news.

'I'm sorry to put a spanner in the works,' she said rather sheepishly, 'and perhaps I should have mentioned this before, but the vast majority of these frogs are hermaphrodite and the pheromone trail won't be strong until they reach maturity which lasts for about an hour. So, um, the bait might need changing every other hour.' Silence. 'Also, I'm not sure we can agree to keeping them in a cage. So this probably won't work.'

The chair, in a dark pinstripe, greying round the edges and introduced to the meeting as Graham, sighed. A gentle sound, which may have indicated defeat but somehow implied that another four hours would be thrown at the problem before admitting it.

'Back to the drawing board then.'

* * *

Alex's second seat had been an eye opener. In the planning team she's the only trainee, unlike in commercial litigation where she had Chris and Carla for company. It was a different world, not just in terms of the work but in the whole dynamic of the department. She'd expected an induction in some form; some sort of who's who or what's what. Instead she found herself in a seemingly forgotten end of the top floor of the building, surrounded by files and reading an email that simply said, 'Everyone out of the office today. List of things to do below. Presume you have handover note from Erin Davis for background. Nice to have you on board.' It was perfectly pleasant, but a little odd to be the only person there, trying to make sense of a new field. And the handover note…!

Erin emailed it on Friday evening, the very last thing before all trainees in the firm moved departments like professional speed-daters. Alex had spent the afternoon packing her folders into the large blue crate provided – books, pens, photos, all the trinkets with which she'd decorated her desk followed – and writing her own handover note, so she hadn't seen Erin's effort until Monday morning.

Erin clearly wanted to be as helpful as she could (she was moving into her fourth seat and wanted to impress) and the note was enormous – when Alex eventually worked out the name of her new printer, with only three calls to IT, the hard copy reached 20 pages. What it didn't have was any information about where Alex needed to start, just an endless and alphabetical list of all the jobs Erin was currently working on. Alex thought back to her own handover; she'd tried her best to prepare the incomer for Nathan, but most of what she needed to say she decided to discuss face to face. She didn't want to write down impressions, especially over email or, worse, via the messaging system the firm operated. She'd put her jobs

SEAT 2: PLANNING

down in order of priority with a list of the immediate steps to take to move each file on. When she'd read it back, she tried to put herself in the new trainee's position – would it make sense if you didn't have the context? She thought it did. Then the emails began.

Being the only trainee in the department was, she quickly learnt, hard. It wasn't so much the amount of work, rather being the focus of everyone's attention. It felt, even on that first day, as though she was the pivot around which everything moved. She was needed by everyone, and it made her feel important – and exhausted. The hours were long, and the demands overlapped – a report for one of the three partners; a draft planning obligation agreement for another; attending calls for the two associates and writing the minutes; producing a daily email of client-related work that made the papers – often the papers, often the legal press but sometimes more widely. This was something Erin had got right: top of the list, in bold, was the legend, 'It's your responsibility to send round the client email – spend an hour in the morning running through the client list and provide links to any developments in the press. Danielle loves it and will notice it, even if no-one else does.'

Danielle (Danny) Western, the youngest of the three partners in the department, was known not to mince her words. Still, Alex was pleased to be working with her. She had a reassuring presence and other trainees, including Erin, had said that she took appraisals really seriously; she seemed to really care about your progress. Better than that, she had a dry wit that seemed to baffle most people, but which made Alex smile behind her hand most days Danny was in the office. So, the client update got lots of attention, and as she got more familiar with the client names Alex began to enjoy the hour in the morning she spent researching, beginning to provide comment on some of the more interesting developments.

Her diligence paid off. One Friday, a couple of months into the seat she happened to notice a report in *The Times*. A major relief road was planned and an environmental consultation required. It was a brief article which caught Alex's eye mainly because of its proximity to her hometown. As she read it, she recalled a client who was considering a bid in that area, mentioned at a team meeting. She wondered whether it was worth noting and decided it merited a mention at the end of the daily briefing, just in case some of the team were interested.

Danny was. Later that morning Alex's phone rang.

'I was pleased to see you'd spotted the environmental stuff in Dewsbury. Funnily enough, I've just been instructed on that one – I'd like you to help out. Can you tell the rest of the team so that they understand you might have limited capacity for a bit?'

* * *

Weeks turned quickly to months, as the bypass matter progressed. It was fascinating – so much work for one five-mile stretch of road – culminating in two key meetings. A final meeting to approve plans for the road was dramatically taken in a different direction when a local environmental pressure group introduced evidence that the pool frog, extremely rare and astonishingly sensitive to any sort of habitat change, was present in large numbers and the road would bisect their land. It was that evidence which led to the meeting with the Frog Lady on a wet morning in March.

Danny and Alex, acting for the local council, had been tasked with putting together a paper detailing solutions used or suggested before. It fell to Alex to trawl through planning decisions: a bat corridor, a turtle enclosure, a newt tunnel, to summarise the options and the legal basis for documenting them, with the resulting paper forming the agenda at the meeting.

Danny had looked at Alex's summary and, to her pleasure, made very few changes to the legal elements (although did remind her of house style and making sure she consistently used defined terms). She'd found that in this seat she had less direct client contact but that the team was much more reliant on the work she produced. Regularly her work was sent out with little to no amendment, which brought its own worries about whether the work was correct but generally was immensely satisfying.

'All this fuss for some frogs,' Danny grinned as she drove alarmingly close to the campervan in front. 'It's probably added a hundred grand to the process.'

Alex, who'd spent the last two weeks preparing bundles of documents for the meeting and had read more about the pool frog than she would ever be called upon to know, made a sympathetic noise.

'It's not their fault that a road's about to be built over them. Apparently it's the biggest colony in Europe.'

Danny inclined her head. 'You know if this goes ahead, it'll make the national press? It's never been done before – formally, in a planning app, I mean.'

Still, getting to that headline meant finding a solution to the tunnel tempting conundrum. 'I wonder,' Graham tells the meeting, 'whether food, rather than a female frog, would do the job just as well.' As one, they turn to Frog Lady.

'Well… it wouldn't have quite the same…' she hesitated, searching for the right word, 'potency. But it could work.'

* * *

Two months later, presentations made, planning approved and tunnel authorised, the relief road makes national news.

'Is that your project?' Carla asks over coffee.

'Yeah, the team's really pleased as we're mentioned as advisors to the council – just in general terms. I can't really ring home with my name in the news.' Alex grinned. 'Still, fantastic to work on.'

'One for the CV! Sounds like you enjoyed the seat…?'

'I really did. Great people and I liked the work, but I think the team's just a bit too small for me. It's made me realise how much I like working with the junior lawyers. Also, it's full on all the time and I wonder if I'd get on better doing something that's a bit more up and down. You know, less of a constant grind! What about you?'

Carla nodded as she sipped her coffee. 'Yeah, I feel that way too. I really enjoyed my corporate seat – it was really intense at times, working all night, but then once the project completed and everything was signed there tended to be a bit of come-down time where everything got finalised and sent out to the client and you could ignore the phone for a while. I might qualify there, if they'll have me. And interview permitting.'

'Still seems a long way off,' Alex said thoughtfully. 'Mind you, the year has disappeared. We'll be done as trainees before we know it.'

* * *

Back at her desk and Alex reviewed a documents list for the relief road matter. The list ran to 10 pages, the production process has been laborious and, unusually in Alex's brief experience, the documents were signed in hard copy rather than via DocuSign software.

The sun streamed through the window and Alex tried to keep her mind on the task, her feet on the box of confidential waste that she'd put out for shredding that morning. It had been a good day – Danny had emailed the whole team commenting on the relief road being covered by the national news and had mentioned Alex's contribution specifically. She'd got some really positive emails in return from others in the team, something that meant a great deal given some of the inevitable politics around her deep involvement in the matter.

In another positive, Danny was going to do her appraisal together with her supervisor: she'd written down in some detail all the things she'd been responsible for, expecting it to be just her and her supervisor, and in case Danny didn't have time to provide feedback, but it sounded as though that wasn't going to be necessary now (although it would still be useful when she wrote up the appraisal on the internal system). She'd lifted most of it from her reflection journal anyway.

The satisfied feeling began to leave her, and a cold grip took hold of her stomach. Where was document 12? She went back through the pile, moving to the next desk so she could separate everything out. She took each of the signed copies and lined them up on the desk, edges touching, hoping to bring order to the chaos. She'd been so careful! 11…13, but no

12 on the desk, in the binders, in the crates used to move signed copies around. The tightness rose – her throat felt like it was closing and she was breathing a little harder. Where the hell was it?

A rustle from the end of the office brought her back and when she looked up she saw a flash of blue disappear behind the kitchenette as the recycling was emptied. It took a moment for the synapses to fire, to think it through, and she had to sit down. When she'd come back from the meeting, full of the confidence of a job done well, she'd added the bundle of unused papers to the recycling box under her desk. There were printouts of documents that had subsequently been changed, notes scribbled on rough paper – one of the clients had left a notebook full of verbatim notes of the negotiations in a careful and huge cursive (that he'd obviously written out just to pass the time, leaving it on the table, once done, with a 'You have confidential waste, right?' in her direction). She'd had an armful of that stuff, now long gone given the weekly collection was the evening before. She made a futile call to reception.

'The confidential recycling – when's it collected?'

'It goes the same evening, so the last one would have been yesterday. We could call the company and see if they can stop the load, but we'd have to pay for the delay. Is it urgent?'

Was it urgent? It was an internal document – something that changed internal permissions dealing with signatories – and Alex suspected they could get another signed. On the other hand, the client (the corporation, not the people) wouldn't acknowledge any of this unless the signatories lined up internally. Legally, the deal was done, but given the client was heavily regulated, mistakes with signatories would lead to extremely unwelcome questions about how the deal was signed off. If not a disaster, this would be an embarrassment.

Alex could see the disappointment, could feel her chances of qualifying into the department disappearing. It had gone so well and now some stupid mistake threatened it all. She wasn't even sure that she wanted a career in this area but it was too early for doors to close. She sat, staring at the backlit screen, eyes unfocused and thoughts elsewhere. There was nothing to do but to tell Danny. The sick feeling came again, with a pressure in her head that made her feel as though she'd never have a coherent thought again.

***

Danny laughed.

'You've managed to shred an original?'

The laughter was unnerving. Was it criticism? Disbelief? Some sort of contained fury? Danny was still looking at her screen, seemingly unconcerned, finishing an email although she'd waved Alex on to speak from half behind the cabinet she peeked around, as though keeping it between her and Danny would lessen the damage.

'I didn't mean it – I'm SO sorry. I know I should have checked I had all the originals before getting rid of anything. I thought I'd contact the client…'

The laughter stopped, but when Alex looked up, the eyes twinkled.

'First, it's not the end of the world: it's an internal thing that we can sort out directly with the client. It doesn't involve the regulator. It could have been worse. It sounds like you've learnt the lesson – and believe me, you'll never throw anything away again after this without checking and double checking.'

Alex let out a long breath. There was a pause.

'How do you think we should fix it?'

'I'll email to say that the document's been misplaced, but that we'll courier over a replacement for them to sign,' Alex suggested.

'Well, I'd start with a call.' Danny leant back in her seat. 'Make sure you apologise of course, but stress that this doesn't impact on the work done. Then we can send over a replacement. Have you got a certified copy?'

'No, I didn't get a chance…' Alex's voice quivered at the confession. Danny held her gaze for a beat, appraising.

'You've done well in this seat, Alex, I mean, you've been balancing all sorts of competing demands from everyone – juggling lots of balls. I'm

SEAT 2: PLANNING

not saying this because you've made a mistake. They happen – it's how you deal with it which marks you out as someone with the competencies we want. You came to me quickly and we can sort this out. But I know how quickly and easily one can become disillusioned with an area and I wouldn't want you to discount us. I think you work well and seem to enjoy this bit of the law and you should think seriously about pursuing it.'

* * *

'That was good of her to say,' Carla said between sips of latte.

The new version of the document had been sent and signed, the client equanimous about it, as the project leaders had already moved on to new transactions and the internal legal team understood it was process only. A close call.

'Although a bit close for comfort...' reading her mind.

'You have no idea – I was...' Alex tailed off, but Carla was already nodding.

'Bricking it, I know. Look, don't worry too much about it – have I ever told you about a friend of mine and the formal written warning...?' and the story continued for the duration of their coffee.

Although Alex knew that people had done far worse and survived, she recognised the lesson. Nathan's pointers about attention to detail had served her well in this seat and this unpleasant business had reinforced the message. Confronting it head on meant that the uncertainty was brief and the solution swift.

At least, she knew, she could put it to one side and see the seat for what it was: a successful one, full of interesting, topical work and a team she enjoyed working with. She still wasn't sure that it was for her – two seats in meant that there was lots more to experience to see if it 'fit' her. She looked forward to the corporate M&A seat coming next, although she'd heard the hours were long and the clients rather unforgiving (which clients weren't, she wondered).

Carla (of course) had given her chapter and verse on the challenge.

'Go to all the socials – they're big on socials and it'll be noticed if you don't go. And you can come in a bit later – they're not early risers but they tend to stay later (all linked I suppose). Oh, and there'll be a lot of bibling. So, no more binning the original, ok?'

Alex smiled. 'I'll do my best…'

8 | SUPERVISION

In this chapter we will investigate the role of the supervisor – the person who in each seat is entrusted with your 'supervision'.

What does that mean? Well, unfortunately it can mean very different things to different supervisors, so being prepared for an uneven experience will stand you in good stead. Generally, supervision includes taking responsibility for your work (checking it, catching mistakes), your welfare (in terms of work/life balance) and ensuring you learn something during the seat. What many trainees struggle with is the discovery that supervisors will be busy with their own careers and – rightly or wrongly – active supervision may come a (firm) second. Despite the title of this chapter it is once more all about you: how will *you* interact with your supervisor to try and get what you need from them?

We have already looked – in earlier chapters – at when you are likely to first meet your supervisor and how you might approach your work generally (remember, enthusiasm is key). In this chapter we will take some time to examine supervision in more detail: why the supervisory system is as it is, what is expected of a supervisor, and what you can expect in reality. We will discuss what might constitute 'good' or 'bad' supervision and, most importantly, the approach you can take to working with a supervisor to get the best out of them.

The relationship is unique in professional life (aside, perhaps, from between pupil and pupil supervisor at the Bar). It includes elements of teaching, pastoral responsibilities, career guidance, friendship but also, in its simplest guise, simply a junior employee doing work for a senior. At its optimal level there is mentorship – your supervisor not only allows you to grow as a lawyer, but inspires you to do so.

Most people choose their mentor. That isn't a luxury you will have in training. Instead, you'll be allocated supervisors, one for each area of law you practice and they are likely to be of varying seniority. The responsibility for making your supervisor the mentor you need (or at least giving them the opportunity to be the most help to you they can be) will be yours not theirs – it is you that will be moving through the department and it is your career at stake. How you might attempt this is the subject of the majority of this chapter.

Before that, let's consider the role of supervisor closely.

Role of the supervisor

In the recent past, trainees were the preserve of partners or senior associates who would be allocated 'their' trainee. As we saw in Chapter 1, this involved – and frequently still involves – sitting at a desk in the corner of that senior person's office and waiting to be spoken to. Poor Bob Cratchit, crouching over a single candle! In fact, this is surprisingly effective. Much can be learnt from sitting in on (or rather not being able to escape) meetings and calls held in that confined space. This model is slowly being supplanted by a more expansive approach, driven by the trend towards open-plan working. Trainees now tend to sit together, or at least with members of the wider team, and not necessarily near to their designated supervisor. Trainees are a shared resource, available for work with all members of the department. (Some US firms, I understand, have an entrepreneurial training scheme where juniors seek out and benefit from their own work. This is atypical in the UK so I'm not going to consider that aspect of traineeship. It demonstrates, however, the evolving role of the trainee.)

In this situation, your supervisor will be primarily responsible for ensuring you have work to do, but it may not be theirs and they may not be familiar with it. They will remain your first port of call for advice and will carry out your appraisals. This doesn't mean that the relationship is any less important, quite the opposite, but it does mean that from a geographical/physical proximity point of view you are not quite so joined at the hip. As you're now at the mercy of the rest of team, who will all be in a position to give you work and will be eager to do so, your supervisor is not just a source of advice and work, but also a shield against becoming overwhelmed.

This approach brings its own advantages. Rather than being captive, left to do work if and when your supervisor has some to give you, you get to work with the entire team. And working with people, as we will see in Chapter 9, exposes you to a broader scope of work and different ways of working. This is much more effective in bringing practice to life.

Another consequence of this democratisation of trainees is that your supervisor may no longer be a partner or a senior. Mid-level associates (say four to six years qualified) are now regularly given trainees to manage. Whether this is your experience will depend on the size of your team and any internal policies, but a common approach in commercial firms is for a mid-level lawyer to take the lead on supervision, with a partner or a senior associate in the background to introduce the trainee to additional work and to attend and lend authority to appraisals.

Again, I think this works rather well. It means you will always have work to do (four years PQE onwards is the powerhouse of fee-earning work) on behalf of someone sufficiently junior to be approachable. At the same time, the involvement of a senior means you have access to experience and, importantly, someone with whom you can discuss your plans for qualification.

All that said, the general principle is simply that whoever supervises you will need to be of a sufficient level of experience such that they can properly instruct you – it's no help to you or the team if work you do goes uncorrected. You will learn nothing. Your supervisor should be someone who is sufficiently senior and capable to give you work, to review that work and to contribute to the learning of your trade. This is the basis of the requirement that supervisors are properly skilled with a view to passing on their knowledge and experience.

Individual supervisors won't be able to teach you everything – even if they think they can. Variety is a great thing and experience of the differing ways in which senior people work will really help you when dealing with clients. But each supervisor should take the time to teach you *something*.

Many supervisors see trainees as there to do some of the easier tasks and no more; better supervisors will understand that you are bright, willing and eager to learn and will give you more testing work to see what you can do; the best supervisor will see the relationship as reciprocal, one of balance where they receive assistance and in return offer guidance on how you approached and dealt with that work.

It can be easy to fall into the sort of relationship with a supervisor where they – senior and experienced – tell you to do something and you – just beginning your journey – obey. It shouldn't be like this: mindless and lecturing. A colleague like any other, there should be open dialogue with your supervisor about the work, their career and your career. Even, and it happens, when relations sour or there's a clash of personalities there is still much to be learnt from listening to and assisting your supervisor, if only to work out how you might do things differently.

Opening and maintaining that dialogue isn't easy. To help you do this, later in this chapter I set out the PAL System – a method for making sure that you and your supervisor communicate regularly and understand one another. Before we get to that, let's take a look at different styles of supervision.

'Good' and 'bad' supervision

It's reasonably well accepted that a 'good' supervisor is someone who describes the nature of the work fully and gives clear instructions. They provide:

(i) Suitable context and background, setting out the origins of the project or matter, the characters involved and a potted history of the client relationship. This might be very short if it's an easy one-off task or it might be a couple of hours if it's a complex matter that's been running for some time.

(ii) Detailed instructions about what you need to do, including where you might look for answers, who you might talk to and what the resulting product should look like.

8 | SUPERVISION

(iii) A process of review and comment on the work you ultimately produce. In other words, they fully embrace the teaching aspect of their role.

A 'bad' or unhelpful supervisor could be characterised as someone who gives you very little or nothing to work with:

(i) Flicks on an email chain with a 'please deal…' at the top and no context. It happens more than you think.
(ii) Gives no further instructions and provides no opportunity to ask questions.
(iii) When you ultimately send some work, gives no feedback or even fails to acknowledge you have responded.

Perhaps it is self-evident that these are two extremes of supervision and one approach is more helpful than the other. Yet I hope it is also clear that for you to get the most from the relationship there must be constant engagement and reflection. There is a tension here between the quality of being independent and using your initiative versus being available to respond to the requirements and needs of your supervisor. Preference for style of supervision will differ – some of you will want more advice than others – and supervisors will be busy people, only able do what time allows. In short, there will need to be contributions from both you and your supervisor to ensure the relationship works. One method for building this regular interaction is to use the PAL System.

The PAL System

I'm happy to admit that the acronym accounts for ninety percent of my pleasure in using this approach, but as forging a relationship with your supervisor is a necessity, why not make them a friend? Making your supervisor a PAL is most likely where you *Prepare* for conversations and work, *Acknowledge* your role in the work to be done and *Listen* to (or *Learn* from) the instructions given, sources suggested and clarifications made. Let's break that down.

Prepare

The training process is all about making you a competent independent lawyer. That means paying attention to *how* other people do things not just *what* they do or ask you to do, readying to make your own judgements about how best to interact with clients and advise them in the context of our service industry. Providing that service, which is at the heart of what we do, begins by assisting your supervisor in their work, giving them support in return for helping you learn the ropes. And you provide this assistance in the best way possible by preparing. That's easy to say but what does it actually mean?

Although there's no magic implied, 'preparation' here goes much further than basic completion of your research or being in a position to provide verbal feedback when asked. 'Preparation' in this sense indicates a general mindset: whatever you are asked to participate in, be prepared.

Let's say you are asked to attend a call in a partner's office. I have every faith that you will be able to get to the right room, on time and with paper and a pen (or – let's get $21^{st}C$ – your laptop/tablet). But being prepared goes further than that. Do you know:

(i) The dimensions of your role – will you be expected to take formal minutes or just some general notes? To repeat myself, always assume that you are taking notes unless told otherwise. Stories abound of trainees coming out of meetings and being asked to send round notes to the participants only for a sheepish admission that there are no notes and no record of who attended;

(ii) The subject matter of the meeting;

(iii) Whether there's anything you need to read in advance, either to actively contribute to the meeting or just to make it easier to understand the discussion. 'Making it easier to understand the discussion' doesn't mean you have spent days researching the relevant law – let's leave the legal stuff to the side for now – rather that if you understand who is attending, from which stakeholder, and the proposed subject and nature of the discussion, then it will be vastly easier to carve out a narrative when you are inevitably called upon to write something up.

This simple idea carries disproportionate rewards. Your supervisor has given you some work; you don't understand it and want to ask some questions. Prepare. Sit down and try and put into your own words what you think you have been asked to do – it's going to help you to reflect what the task is at the beginning of the session. Then consider the questions you have: you already know that there's a general point you don't follow, but do you have other, specific queries? You've finally got their attention – make sure that you are ready to cover all the ground you need to. Bring the document so you can look at the wording together. Write a little crib sheet if you need to. Prepare.

You've been asked to accompany someone to a meeting. This time, again, let's assume we have the 'when' and the 'where' covered, but it's external: do you need to ask someone for access to the building? What about documents? Even if your supervisor hasn't mentioned it, they might be thrilled if you turn up with a bound set of papers ready for review by all parties (or have them downloaded so that you can pull them up on your laptop or tablet quickly). Check what's required of you in terms of getting ready for that meeting. That, in itself, is the Preparation mindset. (Just be careful with taking the initiative too far as unrecoverable and unnecessary costs can be a sore point.)

Acknowledge

Ok, so we're prepared. But lawyers are only human (despite all the jokes) and notwithstanding all your efforts to get a grip on what your supervisor's asking, it just isn't clear. This will happen all the time. Your supervisor is likely to have been working on the project for a significant amount of time before you become involved – what is obvious to them may make no sense to you without context. It may be that you can't even give the benefit of the doubt. With the best will in the world, some people, however senior (even *because* of that seniority) find it impossible to express themselves clearly. Others simply don't know what they want the result to be and the purported 'instructions' are really just suggestions of places to start. Acknowledgement is all about establishing to your satisfaction what has been requested and the expectations for your output, answering the question: 'What do you want from me?'

This is a bilateral exercise. Your supervisor may not be looking at it in these terms but, using your understanding of the Acknowledge step, you should be able to lead them to a place where both of you are happy that clear parameters for the work have been set. It's as much in their interests as yours.

Before we look at different ways to approach the Acknowledge step, let's be clear: there will always be things you don't understand or follow when you are given a piece of work. Never fear, this happens to everyone. It will continue to happen to you until you are a partner, where it just happens more. Clients don't know what they want and can't explain it in legal terms and so you will be taking shots in the dark quite a lot of the time. Treat interactions with a supervisor who has difficulty expressing themselves as practise for dealing with a difficult client – one who needs your help but can't quite vocalise why.

How to start: you are trying to establish what's expected of you, so begin by acknowledging the task and repeating back to your supervisor the instructions they've given. Clarifying the question in the same terms it has been posed forces the person giving that instruction to consider whether it is intelligible. Write it down. At this point you have tacitly agreed with your supervisor that 'this is the task' – whether this makes sense to you at this point is irrelevant as you can go away and research it. If you don't understand at that point, don't despair, you have acknowledged that there is a question that needs answering and the terms of reference for that question and that is half the battle.

Once you have clarified the task (at least in the terms in which your supervisor is willing to give it), start to unpack the practicalities: when is it needed by? How should it be presented? Do you need to include input from anyone else? This is the second stage of Acknowledge step: by asking practical questions about delivery of the work you are acknowledging that this is a service industry regulated by client requirements and therefore the timetable for, and format of, advice is crucial information.

You are also able to acknowledge, at this stage, other pressures on your time. If you have work to do for other people in the department then you can mention this will (or may) impact on your ability to deliver. This is managing expectations and shouldn't be seen (or taken) to be a negative – as we have already touched on, be enthusiastic about the work (see Chapter 5) but be clear about any limits. Taking the discussion in this direction gives the opportunity for both you and your supervisor to acknowledge the restrictions within which the work is to be produced.

Listen

Where have we got to? We've prepared our questions, we've acknowledged the scope of the work. Hard on the heels of all that communication, the third step is to listen (and learn).

Following the Acknowledgement process, your supervisor will have advice for you, suggestions of how to find answers, requirements for how work is presented. However, there's no guarantee that they will present these things neatly – they are busy people and may or may not have the desire or the skill set to teach (whatever we think the truth of the role should be). So, the first limb of listening – obvious as it may be – is to soak everything up. Write down as comprehensively as you can everything that you are told at the beginning of a job; you won't have the perspective or the understanding to know what's important and it almost certainly won't be set out in a tidy chronology, so write down as much as you possibly can for review at a later date.

Listening, as with Preparation, is more than just taking dutiful notes and paying attention to what has been said. It involves finding the nuances: are there particular things that your supervisor likes? Worse, hates? Everyone has bugbears. One person might find it irritating not to be given a hard copy of a paper you have written, another might find it completely unnecessary for you to waste printer ink in the digital world. Clearly there will be more important issues, but paying attention to the small stuff is the quickest way to learning what your supervisor requires of you.

Does it sound as though there's little room for you to take your own approach to work? That isn't the case. Discovering the lawyer that you are is a fundamental part of the trainee experience. Remember, though, it's not just the law you're picking up but the attitude and the culture of the team you're in. Listening to and learning from your supervisor is going to give you the best insight into that tone.

Application of PAL

Let's apply PAL.

As we saw in Seat 1, Alex experienced a particularly difficult interaction with her supervisor. To recap: Nathan leaves a memo on her chair relating to a filing which needs to take place as soon as possible, with the infamous sign-off 'Failure to complete this will be a career limiting move'. Now, while this exchange isn't in any way enlightening from a 'how to approach the task' perspective, and Alex experiences a moment of terror given the gravity of the task and the limited nature of the instructions, this is not as desperate a situation as it might at first seem.

For a start, the instructions are written so Alex can read and digest them. Second, her supervisor is out for the rest of the day meaning that should other members of the department be amenable, there will be time to go and discuss the issue with other people. Third, Alex *understands* that it is a significant task.

Fitting that into our PAL approach, we can say that:

(i) There is time to Prepare and Alex needs to do so – she must be clear about what she understands the task to be, what information she has or can find out and what further information she needs. Following this preparation, she can then…

(ii) Acknowledge the work. Let's say that she has found what she needs to file but is not clear how the firm's internal procedures allow her to do so, she could email Nathan along the following lines:

'Nathan – many thanks for your note. I have spoken to other members of the

team and I can concentrate on completing this for you today. I have found form X and I will complete it and ask Maria [the senior associate who is in the office and has familiarity with the client] to check it this morning. I will need to get in touch with Contact Y [the firm's court clerk liaison officer] to make sure I can make the filing alone – I will update you as matters progress.'

Where instructions are (or seem) incomplete, setting out clearly the task you think you are undertaking together with the steps you will take to complete it allows you to clarify your thoughts and permits those supervising you to confirm or correct your approach – it is Acknowledgement in action.

(iii) Finally, Alex must be sure to Listen and adjust. If Maria tells her: '*I spoke to the client late last night and I'm not sure they need this anymore as their internal team made the filing*', then Alex should not continue. But remember: she shouldn't be passive. She still needs to lead – the responsibility remains with her. She could email Nathan, copying in Maria, politely checking the instructions have indeed changed. If Nathan is unavailable, she will need to consider a polite confirmatory email to the client, something that is good practice in any event.

The point is that even when supervision is poor – and be in no doubt that the initial exchange between Nathan and Alex is not how to do it – there is something to be learnt if you keep your eyes and ears open and allow the process to guide you into good habits.

What are you able to control?

Even using PAL, your relationship with each supervisor will be complicated and unique. There are many factors at work: your respective personalities; the way each of you prefers to work; the type of work involved; the frequency and intensity of supervision (offered or preferred). It is not possible to control everything. Yet as we have seen, there are a number of factors that you *can* control.

Be what your supervisor wants you to be. If they are very busy, then the work needs to be as accessible and complete as it can be before you approach them. You may need to schedule appointments to go through work; if so, come prepared with multiple questions on various matters and make the time count, don't spread things out. If your supervisor likes the detail, give it; if they only want the answer, give the answer and reserve the detail in case they want to discuss it further. Tailor your work to your audience.

Communicate. As we have discussed, you are balancing being self-sufficient with ensuring you get attention and the best way to do that will depend on your personalities and, to some extent, the administrative requirements of your organisation. Passivity is likely to go down poorly. Saying that you don't understand a piece of work and need to discuss it in more detail is likely to be much better received than a vague attempt at an answer accompanied by some rather hesitant questions, an approach which undermines any answer you've given by suggesting you didn't really understand the task in the first place.

It's perhaps because law is seen as such an academic discipline that those new to its practice are concerned that they should be able to do fantastic work immediately. Practice is very different to study; answers are needed quickly and precisely and much comes from experience. Questions are therefore an absolute requirement of trainees. Speak up! It demonstrates your active engagement with the job. The trick, if there is one, is to work out how best to ask them. That is where PAL comes into its own.

Perhaps most importantly, and if there is one 'take-away' from this chapter this is it: always emphasise your interests. There is nothing more beguiling than enthusiasm to someone who is trying to teach. Finding something you enjoy and pursuing it will make your training purposeful. This is where communication with your supervisor is paramount – whatever else is going on in the relationship, they are ideally placed to help direct your involvement in the department's work. They are the ones with relationships throughout the team and they will be aware of the pipeline of work to come. Colleagues will also approach your supervisor, who is assumed to have the best knowledge of how much work you have on your plate, to see if they can involve you in projects; your supervisor can make

8 | SUPERVISION

the case for your involvement where you want to join in and shield you (business needs permitting) from being sucked in to projects that have little utility for your training or future direction.

That's not to say you should attempt to block yourself off from new experiences and challenges – that would compromise the conceptual basis of training. But there is no doubt that your supervisor plays a role in whether you spend the week drafting a particularly complex letter agreement or bundling for court.

Supervisors are there to develop you and should be keen to get you involved in the work you actively choose – a willing protégé is the best. So, be vocal about how you want the seat to go and the type of work you'd like to do.

Personality

The key relationship in making your training a success is often said to be the link you make with your supervisor in each seat. As we have seen, this, like most generalisations, contains a grain of truth but doesn't tell the whole story. Yes, that relationship is important in helping you to learn as much as you can and to gain as much experience as you can. It can be pivotal. But the training experience is also teaching you to be self-sufficient – to be able to carry out tasks independently. In some ways, the supervisor is there simply to give you (or rather the client and the SRA!) the confidence that your work is being appropriately reviewed by someone with experience. Working well it should be so much more than that: a dynamic relationship where both individuals grow.

It is rare that the relationship entirely breaks down. Where it does, there can be a feeling of betrayal on the part of the trainee, of trust broken, perhaps stemming from a perceived failure of the teaching role a supervisor is expected to embrace. This is unlikely to be your fault and you are unlikely to be able to fix it; sometimes people just don't gel.

Yet even in the worst situation, always keep trying to build a relationship of some sort. Apply the PAL technique to keep the lines of communication open. If nothing else, sit back and look at the overall approach of that person to their profession and see what you can pick up. What do they do well? What would you do differently? Most clashes are, at root, about personality and style. A supervisor, no matter how ill-fitting for you, will be an experienced professional so there will be much you can still learn.

Takeaways

» Your supervisor can be a mentor, teaching not only the legal ropes but also how to deal with colleagues, clients and progress your career.

» You can have a bad supervisor! They are only human. Clashes are often down to incompatible styles of working on both sides. A bad supervisor still has much to teach you – you may just have to sit back and observe.

» Use the PAL System: it will allow you to get a very clear idea of what you are expected to do (or, alternatively, it will demonstrate to you that the failings are not yours but a result of bad instructions). Keep it up even if you don't get much back. Nine times out of ten this approach should help cement a healthy working relationship with your supervisor, getting them onside for qualification and beyond.

» Take control of the things you can. Don't be passive; try to fit in (within reason) with the way in which your supervisor works and likes things done. Communicate.

9 | YOUR COHORT AND OTHER SUPPORT

People – they're funny, aren't they? Funny, 'ha ha' and funny peculiar, and there won't be anybody you find more peculiar than the people you work with. You'll get to know their quirks and foibles, what they like and what they don't, and who has a novelty mug boasting a picture of their cat's face which 'CANNOT BE USED'. Even with hybrid working, which has impacted on the closeness of working relationships, no question, the regular contact with your colleagues required for legal work means you get to know those in your team very well as they flash up on screen for the fifth time that day. Yes, this will be the side they present professionally, at least to start with, but still that's quite an intimate relationship and something not always appreciated when entering the professional world. (That's also why the social side of professional life is so important, as we see in Chapter 11.)

There shouldn't be anybody in the department or wider office with whom you can't rub along but, as in any close relationship, there will be times when it's all going brilliantly (and you feel as though you've found your tribe) and times when those relationships are put to the test (particularly when you're under pressure).

Personality (reprise)

As we saw in the last chapter, leaving the academic world behind and moving into the legal profession requires an understanding that personalities play a much larger role. The trick isn't to try and satisfy everyone all the time (impossible); rather it's about respecting the different ways in which people work, the ways in which they want things presented, and the types of effort they appreciate.

It's not just me saying this. Have you ever done one of those personality tests that attempts to identify your dominant attributes and categorises you accordingly? You can find them readily online. Firms frequently ask you to do these, not to test your aptitude for the law, but to try to assist teams in managing their behavioural dynamics. For example, if someone is determined to be very rules-based and managerial, they might want to consider softening that default approach with some training on people skills, perhaps seeking to enhance their emotional capital. Someone else may have a conciliatory personality: a people pleaser at the other end of the scale. In that case, they might want to focus on improving their ability to make hard decisions and have difficult conversations.

I'm not suggesting that you need to do any of this in advance of starting your training – although feel free if you're interested. I mention it to illustrate that firms take personality very seriously as a driver of the effectiveness of teams, and therefore the ability of the team to carry out its work competently.

As an aside, I'm not convinced this sort of test is particularly useful, however unbiased they try to be by asking the same question many times in different ways to try and parse the truth. I've been told things that are completely at odds, from one test to another. I may be peculiar, but they should be taken with a definite pinch of salt and are certainly not something to base your career around. Still, if you are asked to take one, it's worth doing as a conversation starter between team members.

More about your cohort

One of the most exhilarating things about starting as a junior lawyer is the people you meet. Of those people, it will be the colleagues in your trainee cohort who will be your mainstay. They will help, inspire, commiserate with, and teach you. They can be a source of support, of healthy competition, of friendship and advice.

No-one else, even the trainees in the intake(s) above you, will be going

9 | YOUR COHORT AND OTHER SUPPORT

through the same experience – market conditions are changeable, the amount of work coming into any given department varies, the personalities change. Not all of you will stay in law and only a very small proportion of you will end your careers as full equity partners (or wish to). But for the time you are together, you are the single most important resource for one another.

Imagine being a junior commercial solicitor, 18 months qualified. You're reviewing a contract which throws up some entirely unfamiliar terms relating to intellectual property (IP). You need to know what they mean.

You could tell the senior person you're working with in your department, who could call their opposite number in the IP department, who could ask a junior to look at it and come back to you, and later that night you may have your answer.

Alternatively, you could pick up the phone to your fellow trainee in the IP team, someone that started on the same day as you, whom you know well. Now, they almost certainly won't have the answer at their fingertips – they are very new too – but they know the department. They can describe who in the team is approachable or they can go and ask the question on your behalf and come back to you more quickly. When you report the outcome to those in your own team, you have demonstrated your self-sufficiency, your initiative and that you understand there are facilities to be used in the firm where questions are outside one's specialism.

All of this depends on you making your cohort colleagues your allies. It is not a competition in any sense. They are your support.

Many firms, although it has become less common in recent years, operate two intakes a year: in September and the following March. It is a wild generalisation, but the March intake may have a different feel to it, catering to those who want to travel or work elsewhere in the gap between completing law school (in whatever guise) and the start of training. This is likely to be diluted by the advent of the SQE, the demise of the LPC, and the availability of disaggregated training. Those who start in September tend (although, as I say, this is far from always the case) to have moved straight from study to practice.

Why point this out? Only to say that this works quite well, giving different perspectives to the two groups. One could characterise the September intake as more immediately career-focused and eager to get going. Those who join in March may have taken some time to do other things before starting work and have stories to share because of it.

By the time you qualify you will have been through the same training, with the same experiences, as everybody else and the distinction I'm drawing in no way impacts on your performance as a lawyer. Being aware of the interests and subtle differences between your colleagues is one way to anticipate ways to engage with them – this is what's important.

You may disagree with this characterisation and, if so, I'd be happy because it means you're paying attention to the people you're meeting and the circumstances in which you find yourself. *That* is the crucial skill: to see yourself as part of the group and the organisation from early on, rather than as a new face waiting for instructions.

Non-fee earning colleagues

It should go without saying that support staff must be treated with respect (as you would any colleague). They are, indeed, likely to be the most valuable relationships you can develop. PAs know the IT systems backwards and can help you with typing, formatting, expenses, all the admin you can imagine. The IT team is there for the inevitable system or document crashes. Your firm's print room can save the day when you suddenly realise you need 20 copies of a 400-page document in the next two hours – although the emphasis on sustainability may mean this isn't as frequent an occurrence as it was. Your innovation and/or legal tech team will be there to help with AI, with a view to working smarter not harder. If these relationships aren't nurtured, life as a trainee can be much more difficult than it needs to be. Yet, unfortunately, some trainees find these the hardest relationships to manage.

I suspect this is because the act of giving someone else something to do on your behalf doesn't come naturally to most of us. At trainee level you are used to being (relatively) self-sufficient students and doing things for yourself. While universities are much more attuned to student needs than they once were, they do not extend themselves to giving you a secretary! Trainees generally seem to react to that relationship in two ways: (1) they don't use the resource, seeking to avoid the PAs (for example) altogether, making professional life far more of a struggle; or (2) unused to the situation, allow their requests for assistance to (inadvertently) become demands.

You may think such a situation is easily avoided by treating people politely. Keep interactions respectful and all will be well! You are both right and wrong: it *is* easy to avoid by being polite, yet people regularly fail to remember this because, under pressure themselves, the first thing to disappear is self-awareness of how they treat others.

Easing your passage through the training experience depends on becoming part of a team. What this 'team' consists of will change: think of it as increasing concentric circles. Your immediate team will include lawyers, PAs, PSLs – all the people in your department. A slightly wider team would include all those who support that department on a regular basis – risk teams/compliance lawyers, IT, legal technology, printing etc. Some departments are part of a group of departments within the firm – say the employment, pensions and share scheme teams – also regarded as a large 'team'. Finally, as law is an adversarial profession, we can characterise the firm as a 'team' against other firms. This includes the cleaners and security staff who keep the building pleasant and running, allowing everyone who works there to do so in peace.

There is no point trying to separate yourself from your colleagues as you're working towards similar goals and will need assistance at some point during your trainee experience and beyond. Treat people as you would like to be treated. And pay attention to how other people see you behave.

Part of the reason for this – other than being a decent human being – goes back to the importance of reputation (see Chapter 7). Your colleagues will discuss you, your behaviour and your treatment of others, as you will theirs. Politeness begets time and attention; kindness begets kindness. If you are known to treat people well, you will develop a cache of goodwill you can call upon at that moment when you most need assistance – late night help with bundling court documents; a fast-tracked expenses claim; some document formatting and so on.

Office gossip

'Have you dealt with Bob in commercial litigation?', the partner whispered to me. 'Dreadful. Don't know how he got a job. Apparently, he failed to file charges on two separate occasions!'

All offices have a healthy grapevine – it is the way of the world. Office relationships, failures, arguments, disciplinary issues, pay. You name it, rumours will fly and vignettes will be shared over coffee, lunch, an end of the day drink. This isn't necessarily a bad thing: sociologists suggest that a strong interest in those people with whom we spend the majority of our time reinforces the social bond. It's generally no problem and, as they say, today's headlines are tomorrow's fish and chip paper (back when newspaper was used to wrap – yum!).

For poor Bob, two simple mistakes (albeit compounded by making the same error twice), meant word had got around that he was error prone. Doubt about his attention to detail meant his reputation as a lawyer suffered internally.

There are two points to make about this: (1) it is unfair, and the partner should not have been indiscreet, but it happens and there's no point pretending otherwise; and (2) a situation like this can be prevented.

As we saw in Chapter 6 – although it bears repeating – always own up to mistakes quickly and clearly. It happens to absolutely everyone. Legal work is the management of risk and, where an error has been identified, a tweak to that risk profile is often easily achieved with a simple acknowledgement of the position everyone intended.

Mistakes are one thing. They are inevitable in a professional environment and can (and should) be managed. Your reputation will not suffer simply for making an error. However, it will suffer – and this is where you can actively manage matters – if you do not make every effort to present yourself and your work professionally.

9 | YOUR COHORT AND OTHER SUPPORT

To do that, remember Cheerful Working. The firm is an integrated unit; although people will have specific roles and particular tasks, each individual contributes to the whole. The moan about Bob almost certainly has nothing to do with his previous mistakes and everything to do, rightly or wrongly, with a perception that he would not be a help but a hindrance to the *task at hand*.

As we noted in Chapter 5, when you are asked to assist, there will be times when you need to push back and say that you can't carry out a task, perhaps because you don't have available time or you, in good faith, think it should be someone else's responsibility. Yet, most of the time the work will be yours and doing it to the best of your ability and cheerfully is a choice you make. Doing it with a smile is nine-tenths of preserving that reputation.

The most regular office gossip will come from your fellow trainees. Again, this is understandable as you and your contemporaries want to discuss the workings of the firm, the approach taken to supervisors and other employees, and (legal) likes and (legal) interests. Yet, sometimes, it is the relationships and communications with your fellow trainees that take the most work, requiring sensitivity and, on occasion, an ability to ignore or manage rising tensions.

When might such tensions arise? As we have already seen, trainees move seats, usually every six months. Firms have various ways of allocating seats, often involving some sort of reference to choices made (and ranked) by you about areas of law you would like to experience. There is no guarantee that you will be given your first choice, and there are generally a lot of background considerations about seat distribution and the needs of the business – discussions you will not be privy to.

Some people, as in all walks of life, will have firmer ideas than others (in this case about what areas of law they want to experience). This can manifest itself in a particularly vocal approach to trying to secure a particular seat. Stories will abound of Jamie managing to have a coffee with the head of litigation or Mo emailing HR to ensure they get a property seat next. Ignore all of this.

You may hear talk of the third seat (or equivalent if your firm works to a different timetable) as the 'golden seat'. You've done at least a year in the firm – assuming a standard training contract – you know the systems, you know how transitioning between teams works, and you're likely to do your most productive work (so the thinking goes). In the fourth seat you'll be looking towards qualification (see Chapter 12) and so may be distracted. Because of that, trainees with a pre-conceived preference for an area of law often look to experience that area in their third seat. Although that seems logical, it's misleading. It may not be possible for you to request any seat, let alone when it falls and, even if you can, that's no guarantee your wish will be fulfilled. The needs of the business will override everything. If you do get the chance to indicate preferences, you might take such received wisdom into account, but don't put too much store by it. Finding work you enjoy doing, whether your first or last seat, is the important thing.

To reiterate, seat allocations are much like a timetable at school. They are dictated by the needs of the firm and availability within teams, not (solely) by the preferences of the trainee. If the commercial property team feels that it needs one more trainee to support its fee earners, a trainee will be allocated regardless of whether anyone has shown an interest in that area. Similarly, if the employment team doesn't feel it has enough work to support more than two trainees, then only two will be allocated. Neither imploring emails nor proposals for mid-morning coffee will change that.

The firm is also under an obligation to ensure that your training is fit for purpose and so there will be occasions where you'll be required to undertake a particular seat in order to gain specific experience.

That is not to say your requests will be ignored. Law firms understand that engaged employees are more productive and likely to perform better. Having asked you – again, in most cases – to rank your choices, either at the beginning of your training or in advance of each seat allocation, the firm will try to satisfy one of your choices to the extent it can be matched with the needs of the firm.

And there is much to be said for showing interest – a carefully worded email to the head of a department or to the HR team (if your firm has one) or the partner responsible for trainee matters (in the alternative) is acceptable. As I repeat many times in this book, this is the start of your career, and it is appropriate – indeed necessary – for you to take active steps to manage it. That said, you should not be concerned by rumours of other trainees getting preferential treatment or be worried if you are content to follow the suggestions of the firm; influence is limited, and you can be confident that the firm will be doing its best to manage your expressions of interest against the operational requirements of its business.

Credibility

At the risk of labouring the point, it's critical to realise that your reputation will precede you. Your colleagues in your cohort will move between departments in a way that the lawyers don't: yes, they (the lawyers) communicate and do so frequently, but they don't move between teams as the trainees do. As trainees move, supervisors are likely to ask their current trainee for their view of the incoming group. They are also likely to ask their colleagues in the team you've just left.

Now, this is all unofficial and, in the very unlikely circumstances that someone's simply taken against you or it's a seat in which you've underperformed, it won't ruin your career for them to have low expectations. Still, to the greatest extent possible, I imagine you want to be seen as a competent pair of hands.

That word, 'competent', might sound as though I'm damning with faint praise. 'Surely,' you're thinking, 'I want to be seen as a rising star.' Well, do you? How much do you want to promise in advance versus surpassing expectations in delivery? I'd suggest it's better to be seen as decent and then wow the team with your performance than to be deified in advance. (Don't worry – that really won't happen.)

Whatever your thoughts on this, the point is there will be discussion about who you are and what you've done *before you reach the team* and members of your cohort will make a hefty contribution to that conversation. So, try your best to provide support to fellow trainees, as well as asking for help. It will be remembered.

BEING A TRAINEE SOLICITOR

Takeaways

» The people who join the firm at the same time as you – your cohort – will be a source of support, advice and (generally healthy) competition. Make sure you get to know them: use them as a resource and look to provide support in turn.

» Treat everyone with respect. Some of your key allies in the tough work of being a trainee will be non-legal colleagues, particularly on the technical side as the influence of AI is felt. Make friends here.

» As in all workplaces, there will be gossip and rumour. Try not to worry too much about elements of competition within your cohort. More is determined by the needs of the business than by trainee desires.

» Reputation is everything. Linked, clearly, to treating people with respect and the concept of Cheerful Working from Chapter 5, try to be self-aware in everything you do. The approach you take to colleagues and how you do the work will come up in conversation. Your reputation precedes you.

10 | CLIENTS

No matter how talented or diligent a lawyer you are, you need a client: someone who has approached the firm with a question to be answered. Clients are the backbone of the job and both the best and the worst of a service career. It will be a client who'll make your day, sending a fulsome email telling you/your seniors what a good job you've done. It will also be a client that will make you despair at their ineptitude, rudeness or general lack of appreciation for the lengths you have gone to.

A former colleague of mine was (accidentally) copied in to an email from a client, sending on internally some work that had been provided by the firm. 'Feedback from the lawyers,' it read, 'mainly dealing with punctuation!'

To the (silently) outraged lawyer this was sacrilege – the time and effort that had gone into making that document the best it could be, not to mention the years of honing skills, had been completely overlooked in one dismissive aside. Yet, it's a truth we must recognise: legal advice is something thrust upon a client who is otherwise engaged in business or has been accused of a crime or has a family dispute or wants to set up a trust. Whatever the circumstances, the purchase of legal advice is seen by most as a requirement – not something they are particularly interested in, not something to be appreciated as an art, but a service to be provided to limit or manage risk.

Standing back, I'm sure we can all appreciate that position. In fact, it's helpful to put yourself into that frame of mind when you're dealing with clients for the first time.

You will hear people talking about 'adding value'. We touched on this often used phrase in Chapter 4. Most people use it as shorthand for impressing a client: what more can we do beyond providing the legal advice (taken as read) to demonstrate to the client that we're actively managing the project and/or offering additional commercial assessment in our advisory role? For present purposes, the terminology is useful as it fits in well with Cheerful Working, reputation management and extending your willingness to help colleagues or clients. Unfortunately, clients won't notice the legal skills unless the advice provided is wrong, and that may not come to light for some time (see Chapter 6 for how to cope with mistakes), or controversial. They *will* notice immediately your tone, your efforts to co-ordinate internal advice and your presentation of it in an accessible manner.

Your approach to clients: what do they want?

A story (possibly apocryphal) used to go around the City: a senior partner when asked what they were looking for from a potential trainee at interview answered, 'Someone I can leave with a FTSE 100 CEO for ten minutes and, when I return, still have a client'.

Ok, charm is nice to have and being able to present yourself professionally is crucial, but there is more to this. Part of your learning journey is to work out how to address different clients and establish what they need (which is not always what they say they want). How to be formal, but not too formal. How to provide the 'right' advice i.e. the requisite level of detail required *by that client*, presented in a way that is easily digestible *by that client*. It will be bespoke. This is as much a part of what you are learning as the legal knowledge and practical legal skills you will pick up, and there is real advantage to you in recognising these nuances early on and adapting your behaviour appropriately. You will need a level of self-awareness for this.

How you approach clients will necessarily vary depending on the field you're in. Clearly, if you are training (or about to train) at a criminal law firm, your approach to clients will differ hugely from trainees at a corporate commercial firm. Family law focused firms will require different skills again. Yet there are several basic rules about dealing with clients that transcend field.

Confidence. This is difficult to get right. You are unlikely to be entirely comfortable with the material and the advice you are giving in the early days. This is to be expected as it's all new to you. If you feel very confident, you are likely to have faltered on the self-awareness test; if you have no idea what is going on, you run the risk of over-compensating, appearing overconfident, of trying too hard. 'Give us a break!' I can hear you saying, 'everyone puts on a bit of a front'. I accept that criticism. My advice is to regularly reflect on how you come across (and remember my story from Chapter 5 about the interview, where my nerves were interpreted as arrogance). The good news is that it's relatively easy to ensure you present yourself well, sufficient to give the client confidence in you without appearing blasé or over familiar.

Speak directly. Sometimes if you are put on the spot or asked something you don't know there is a temptation to bluster, to talk without knowing quite where you're going or what you want to say. Try and give concise answers, to the point. If you don't know…

Be honest. It is much better to say, 'I don't know the answer to that, leave it with me and I'll go and find out', rather than trying to make it up. Taking a punt on what you think the answer might be is a calculated risk and something that you may be able to get away with as your experience grows. In the early days, however, and this is most of your training, it is a recipe for disaster.

Pay close attention to the client (or the client's representative, if an organisation) as an individual. By this I mean take your cue from the client. Are they talkative? If so, are they looking for responses from you or are they just telling the room about, for example, the state of their business? Have they been discussing sport or their family? If so, that may be a cue for you to take the conversation in a more personal direction. Don't assume this is appropriate without an indication of more. Be sensitive to the expectations of the person you are talking to.

None of this is unique to law or lawyers. It would be applicable in any professional situation. Yet it has an added importance for trainee lawyers because of the structure of the training programme. Other lawyers will understand you are a trainee i.e. that you have probably been in the profession for under two years, moving specialisms multiple times during that period. (I appreciate that those who have been paralegals before moving to solicitor training may have many more years' of experience and that some trainees have had previous careers.) Clients, however, often see no distinction between you and any other lawyer with the effect that the relatively protected role of 'trainee' falls away. In such circumstances you are representing the firm and any comment or impression you give (legal or otherwise) will reflect directly on it.

Alternatively, a client may understand the system of legal training and see you as too junior, generally disregarding your input. This is unfair and extremely rude, but it happens.

In either case, pay attention to our golden rules. In the former situation, where the client hangs on every word, you need to be sure of your material before you advise, so be circumspect and honest about what you can offer. In the latter scenario, you need to read the room. It may be that you try to strike up conversation, find some common ground and if this happens naturally, that's a fantastic outcome. Their initial attitude suggests they won't be amenable to this sort of approach; in that case you need to be sensitive to the client's lead and avoid over-familiarity.

This is not to excuse outright rudeness or worse behaviour from clients. If you feel uncomfortable, talk to your supervisor or the lawyer you are working with.

Building relationships

So far, we have looked at clients from a rather reductive point of view – crudely, how not to irritate them! There is a much richer side to client engagement. Indeed, relationships with clients are, for many lawyers, one of the most enticing things about the profession. Yes, you need to be on your best behaviour as you represent the firm at all times, and you have a duty to act in the best interests of your client, but much of the pleasure of the role is finding the answer to a legal puzzle someone has set you and

10 | CLIENTS

helping them to move forward within that legal framework. That might be expanding their business, solving a personal or family issue, even dealing with the criminal justice system.

The old adage that people buy from people is as true in a legal setting as anywhere else: you will find clients talking about the 'user-friendly' approach of a particular lawyer or the ability to 'turn her hand to anything' and these are all ways of saying in so many words that the lawyer in question was easy to work with, that an approach to working had been established which suited everyone.

Against that background, it should be clear to you that the rules established above (albeit rules in the loosest sense) are built for breaking; they're a starting point only. The important thing is to be sensitive to the needs of the client. As you become sure of yourself, striking up a rapport with the client is absolutely what you should do and what you will spend much of your career attempting to achieve. By building this relationship you can establish how savvy they are: What needs explaining? What level of detail should you provide? How do they prefer to be approached?

It is trite that the ability to give legal advice is a given for the practising lawyer – you will hear this a lot. The real value added (that phrase again) will be the ability to create, on some level, a solution for each client, one that is personal to them.

Some clients might want a one word answer from you, a yes or no. Others might want all the detail and then to discuss the options available. Still others might find legalese (a term for legal jargon) off putting to the point of irritation where another client might want an unusually formal email or paper, full of legal terminology, to show to their board of directors. The possibilities are endless, but the advice is simple: be alert to what the client needs from you.

I should add a brief caveat here, as I did earlier in this chapter. This does not mean you unquestioningly follow client instructions. You are there to assist a client who, by definition, is unfamiliar with the law. You will need to work with them to understand the assistance they require, analysing the facts as presented by them. There are also regulatory demands on you (particularly anti-money laundering requirements and similar that are beyond the scope of this book but in which you will be extensively trained by your respective firms), which may mean you simply can't do something a client wants. You may have to stop acting for some reason. Don't confuse being sensitive to a client's needs with unquestioningly doing what they say.

Emails and tone

To conclude this section, it's worth revisiting emails and tone. We looked at this in Chapters 5 and 8, particularly the potential for emails to signal the experience of the author. Emails will be a primary area for demonstrating client sensitivity as that will be your main method of communication. As we have seen, tone is something you can easily get wrong: too formal or not formal enough; too detailed or not detailed enough.

A favourite story of mine is that of a trainee creating a suite of documents to transfer a shareholding for a knight of the realm. Relentlessly, the trainee copied the client into emailed versions of documents and detailed updates on how the transfer of shares was going. To each lengthy missive, addressed to 'The Honourable Sir X' the response was a simple 'Thanks, and call me Mike'. The trainee worried that calling the client 'Mike' would be much too familiar and insisted on continuing in the original format. This resulted in a complaint to the lead partner. All this client wanted was: (1) to know when documents were ready to be signed, without the detail; and (2) to be called Mike.

This was a minor event, nothing for the trainee to worry about and the client subsequently became 'call me Mike' throughout the department. But it is a neat example of how picking up on and responding to client concerns is, on occasion, much more important to the client than the legal advice (which they will assume a law firm can offer and in which they have little interest).

It is a differentiating factor. The trainee concerned could have deftly adjusted their dealings with the client had they been more alive to the feedback they were getting rather than intent on reporting, formally, the

10 | CLIENTS

legal steps that were being taken in a blinkered way.

You, dear reader, are no doubt academically successful and – assuming you have an offer for training already – have the charm, charisma and commitment to get through a demanding interview with people who see in you the potential to be a fellow professional. You will be capable of dealing with clients and you may find that direct client engagement is the most exciting, perhaps fulfilling, element of a legal career. Maintain your awareness when dealing with clients, as we have discussed and you will succeed, you have my word.

Takeaways

» Reflect on how you come across to clients and be direct and honest about what you know and what you don't. Read the room and take your cue from the client, particularly in respect of moving the conversation in a more personal direction.

» Remember that clients often see no distinction between you (as a trainee) and any other lawyer. You are representing the firm and any comment or impression you give (legal or otherwise) will reflect directly on the firm.

» The adage that people buy from people is as true in a legal setting as anywhere else: striking up a rapport with the client is absolutely what you should seek to do. In doing so, be alert to the needs of the client.

» Picking up on and responding to client concerns, often non-legal, is frequently more important to the client than the legal advice – something they assume a law firm will get right.

11 | FIRM LIFE

Imagine you're six months into training. You have pictures up on your desk, you've changed your screensaver, you've made friends, you've got used to the type of work you will be asked to do and joined more Teams meetings than you have background options. It's all going swimmingly. What next?

Getting involved in the extracurricular efforts of the firm is one of the most rewarding things you can do in your early professional years. There are many ways in which you can get involved, but before we take a closer look at the types of things you could do, perhaps the first question to answer is: what's in it for you? After all, you're trying to juggle various balls at this stage – learning and consolidating new legal skills, working out the sort of professional you are going to be, developing relationships with newly found colleagues. Why, you might fairly ask, would you want to take on further responsibilities?

Getting involved

First and foremost, it can be really enjoyable. As you get involved you will meet a cross-section of the firm, including non-legal staff, consultants, HR and IT, and lawyers of all grades. Extending your internal network this way will be helpful in your future career, and the more people you get to know, the more interesting your working life will be. It's also part of the realisation that your career is shaped by you.

The career opportunities available at any given time will change, and you will be in the best position to identify those which appeal to you – and how you can take advantage of them – by getting out of your immediate department and engaging with others in the firm. Doing so will evidence leadership, teamwork, strength of character, self-sufficiency, many if not all the things you want to demonstrate when you come to apply for jobs at the end of your training. Variety, as they say, is the spice of life and getting involved in the life of the firm beyond the work on your desk, the projects of your team, should be seen as central to your development.

Second, and more prosaically, your contribution to the firm will be something commented upon at appraisal time and form part of your pitch for a job at qualification. Don't be phased by this. It's an opportunity to transfer the skills honed over your university life into the professional world – volunteering, networking, supporting causes, mentoring, sports teams, all of this and more is available to you at most law firms and/or through the local law society. It is an opportunity, not an obligation, and should be treated as such.

Third, most firms will allocate a proportion of target hours to activities beyond the scope of billable work. Involvement in extracurricular activities is something that is anticipated and which counts towards targets (if there are any), so there is no downside to you embracing the offers available.

What's out there?

Let's consider the kind of extracurricular things we're talking about.

Social activities: The most obvious opportunity to get to know people. This may mean drinks organised in your department to celebrate a project completing or the firm-wide Christmas party or a leaving lunch for someone in the team. If you are invited, go. There will be times when you have conflicting plans – life doesn't stop because you've joined a law firm – but by attending these things you will get to see your colleagues in more relaxed surroundings, and you will find that worthwhile.

Corporate Social Responsibility (CSR) or Responsible Business: These are the umbrella names given to efforts by companies, mainly in the private sector, to commit resources to pro bono projects intended to benefit society as a whole. Much of the rest of this list would come under the CSR/responsible business banner; I mention it as you may hear the terms used and wonder what they mean. I'll just refer to CSR going forward, for simplicity.

You may also come across the term 'ESG,' standing for environmental, social and governance factors. In fact, this is probably the dominant term at the time of writing, with CSR taking a back seat, although it tends to remain used by firms to cover things such as volunteering and charitable initiatives, which is why we looked at it first.

ESG as a term emanates from work done by the United Nations, which encouraged people who have a stake or an interest in businesses – in particular, investors and employees in companies – to focus on these issues to create change. They should ask what their company is doing with regard to the environment, examine its social impact (and how that might be measured), and consider whether the company's corporate governance framework (the way in which decisions are made in the company, resulting in its activity), support and enhance those objects.

ESG, then, is a related although fundamentally different idea from CSR. CSR refers to the contribution of the business to society and the environment and the act of seeking to be aware of the impact in doing so. ESG is about overall purpose of the organisation: rather than seeking to do good it should seek to be good, such that the way in which the organisation operates contributes to improvements to environmental and social matters affecting its communities (for example).

I mention this distinction because you may find the terms are conflated at your firm – or that ESG now takes precedence. It's important to know that there is a difference, as they are separate concepts. ESG initiatives often become synonymous with sustainability, so, reducing emissions from the firm's offices and via its suppliers. Still, the opportunities to get involved are likely to be similar: tree planting days, volunteering as a school governor, reading at primary schools and so on, all of which can find a home under either banner.

You may find that firms have moved on from using CSR/responsible business entirely. Many firms are now purpose-led, meaning they try to elucidate why they do what they do – a rallying cry that is intended to be wider than 'to make money'. ESG is frequently mentioned in the same terms, but bear in mind that larger corporate/commercial firms are likely to have an ESG client-facing team which advises on sustainability practices, and, separately, an operational team that looks at the internal activity of the firm (i.e. its environmental impact, its procurement requirements, its modern slavery statement and so on). Be clear about which team you are engaging with.

Pro bono legal advice: Most firms will participate in, or even run, a free legal advice service in some form. Some firms take on clients directly, others participate in clinics run and supervised by an external not-for-profit body. If you're sitting in a contentious team – such as litigation – you may have the opportunity to work on international projects via charities such as Amicus, which works with individuals on death row. Other clinics may be less high profile but equally worthwhile. Disputes about utility bills or other small claims cause deep concern and upset to people, and you can help to steer those individuals in a particular, legally informed, direction.

I'm reliably informed by those working in this area that over the last decade the status of pro bono work has grown rapidly in large firms, at least partially due to wider legal aid cuts. The consequence of this growth has been that pro bono activities have become formalised programmes in which trainees play an important role. You will be able to count some or all of your volunteered time against your targets; indeed, in the largest firms there is often some kind of standalone pro bono target. It may be that your firm offers a secondment to a pro bono client, a charity or a law centre. Firms are keen to support this activity. It develops your independence as an advisor and management will have their eye on the various comparative surveys and rankings available which track pro bono opportunities and contributions made by firms. And it's not just the large operators: smaller firms often provide specific pro bono offers to key clients in the not-for-profit sector or, if a boutique firm, within their specialism.

For those of you whose training is (or may be) at a large corporate firm, this could be the first direct client contact you achieve, and the impact on both you, as the advisor, and the individual you advise will be significant. The person you are assisting, who tells you they've barely slept for a week for worrying about how they will deal with an unexpected and unwarranted £400 electricity bill, will be truly grateful that you listen to and appreciate their concerns. That's before you even get to advice. The advice may be as simple as summarising their problem in an email or letter and finding the right person to contact.

The benefit for you is that not only are you practising all of the skills you need for the day job – interviewing clients, synthesising what they tell you in order to undertake legal analysis, and communicating your conclusions in terms appropriate for that client – you'll also get the satisfaction of making a positive contribution in someone's moment of difficulty and to their experience of lawyers.

As an aside (though an important one), it is vital to ensure you have the approval of your firm and your team in taking on further commitments. This is for various reasons, most of which we have already touched on – concerns around your capacity to do client work, the option to enlist others to help, and being given credit for the additional work you do – but the primary reason is to ensure you are properly covered by the firm's insurance. Whether charging for legal advice or not, if you hold yourself out as a solicitor it is a requirement of the SRA that you are insured (and it is clearly in your interests too). Similarly, if you are volunteering to litter pick along a canal, you will want to be able to rely on the firm's various other insurance policies as its representative. Given what I said about the growth of pro bono work within firms, this is unlikely to be a problem – just something to keep in mind.

Sport: Wherever you practice (geographically), I can almost guarantee there will be a healthy inter-firm sports scene. For those interested, various leagues give rise to (largely) playful rivalry with other firms and provide a good forum for getting to know other lawyers in your area.

Don't dismiss the value of knowing other lawyers. The legal world is a small one meaning you will come up against these people time and again and it's useful to be on good terms. Much like university, there is often funding available to support and encourage sports participation of all kinds (at least in the larger firms).

School support/school governors: Many of the skills developed by trainees, such as a close attention to detail, the ability to write (as 'professional wordsmiths'), the ability to communicate well and to take account of a variety of stakeholders, are transferable. A particular site for use of those skills is education. Many firms acknowledge this and as part of their CSR programmes (by whatever name) encourage lawyers to engage with schools in a variety of ways – taking reading classes, running CV workshops, taking on mentorship roles with older children. For the same reasons, lawyers are in a prime position to assist schools by taking a governing role.

The modern school governor sits on a board of governors that is very close to the board of a company. For those who have been through a corporate seat, the structure and roles of governors and the decisions made about, for example, policies, curriculum and staffing matters will be familiar.

For those who haven't been through a corporate seat, that is no bar. Governors are becoming increasingly professional, and you will be welcomed with open arms with the skills you're learning. In return, involvement in a school will allow you to develop your client handling skills and encourage you to think independently and critically. You'll also get the chance to engage with students via discussions with and presentations by school council (or equivalent), shaping the minds of tomorrow.

Special interest groups: There will be any number of special interest groups that operate in a law firm. Staffed by a bright and high-achieving workforce, there are lots of pet projects that run just for the fun of it. Music is often high on the agenda – choirs, bands, acapella groups – but there might also be drama groups, book clubs and the like. Consider creating your own group if you have a particular interest. There will also be formal or informal employee support groups – LGBTQ+, family and carers, mental health support networks and many more. These are of tremendous benefit and a wonderful opportunity to meet like-minded people or those in similar situations.

Newsletters: Every firm, even the smallest, is likely to have some sort of written all-staff communication, if that only takes the form of shared online workspace. The largest will have some form of employee magazine (available through a cloud-based app, of course). This is the perfect forum for seeing what your colleagues are involved in and/or publicising the groups you attempt to start yourself. If you enjoy writing creatively, this is also a great place to try reportage or, if you're so inclined, to submit travel writing, poetry or anything that you can get past the editorial team! There will be similar publications for different teams based on their areas of expertise or setting out what groups within the firm have been doing in a given sector. Engagement of any sort will be welcomed. For the firm to learn, in an organisational sense, it requires input from its people, the left hand letting the right know what it's doing. Your contribution will help the firm develop for the better.

Leadership roles: My recent professional work has revolved around corporate governance. Whenever I'm speaking about governance to people at the start of their career, I make the point that to create the organisation you would like requires participation and effort. There will always be something that you would like to change or improve, and the most straightforward way to do that is (generally) to work within the existing governance framework. This extends beyond the obvious and senior – the board, heads of departments, team and office leaders – to those groups that help the organisation to operate. So, join an advisory team looking at how to reduce waste, or join a working group considering the contribution AI could make to the business, or join the social committee and plan activities for the firm. These opportunities can be significant and high profile. At least one well regarded firm set up a shadow board of juniors, tasked with advising the main board on points of innovation, utilising the openness to change of a different generation to plug possible blind spots.

Law societies and local business organisations: Almost all firms will be part of a local law society and business community, providing further opportunity to meet your peers in different professions. 'North East Young Business Person of the Year' and similar will be available for you to enter and/or become involved in event planning. While often limited in geographical scope, that doesn't take away from the significant networking opportunity for the local area.

Fitting it all in: the power of groups

These are some of the areas where you could get involved in the life of the organisation, although there will be others depending on the setting of your firm. But how practically do you do this?

To reiterate the point made in the 'Leadership' section above, and as you might have experienced at school or university or through other professional roles you have held, there's a group or a committee for almost everything.

In a law firm most if not all committees dealing with volunteer and social matters will be open to all grades of lawyer and non-legal staff, so you are immediately widening your circle of contacts (and dare I say it, friends) by getting involved. You are likely to be welcomed because, and I must be honest here, organising anything in a work environment can be a thankless task. That is not to say there aren't rewards – this chapter is intended to convince you of the advantages personally and professionally to taking on this sort of role – but it can be burdensome. You will need to make time for meetings, perhaps take minutes, carry out the tasks assigned to you and, obvious but frequently overlooked, attend the event you have organised and sacrifice precious spare time!

And even if this is a wonderful occasion for all colleagues to meet, talk and enjoy themselves, there will inevitably be one or two with 'tips' for how to improve it or who criticise the arrangements. This is par for the course but the benefits far outweigh such frustrations.

Should you discover that there isn't a committee in place to promote an activity/follow leads/plan relevant events, then what better opportunity to begin your proactive involvement? Work out who is in a position to make it happen, talk to them and start the ball rolling. Establishing a formal committee isn't a prerequisite for participation, of course, but given part of your motivation will (or should) be to involve and thereby enhance relationships with your colleagues, some sort of group would be the obvious way to move forward. It also helps to spread the load. Get the word out and, most importantly, have fun with it.

As an exemplar, one of the cherished but truly controversial activities in any organisation is its Christmas party. Whether this is at the organisation or department level, someone will be tasked with putting it together and everyone else (it seems) will take on the role of dissatisfied customer. But no matter: this is a great opportunity for you to get involved and lead from the front. You will have ideas about venues and entertainment that others won't. That band you and your fellow trainees came across at an open mic night – why not recommend them? The pop-up food court in a disused warehouse – is that an option? (Probably not, given Christmas food is sacred.) Is there a good offer for a team Christmas dinner in a local but atmospheric restaurant you've visited recently? Do you know of a venue that offers a delicious vegan alternative?

When the event takes place and, despite the nay-sayers it is a huge success, it is you that your colleagues will thank. Being remembered for your contribution to the team has an impact on your qualification prospects.

Takeaways

» Getting involved in opportunities beyond legal work allows you to meet people who work at the firm in a variety of roles. This helps expand your internal network, while providing a broader understanding of the firm's operations.

» It also allows you to demonstrate leadership, teamwork, strength of character, self-sufficiency, many if not all of things you want to show when it comes to applying for jobs at the end of your training.

» Activities you could get involved in include social activities (participating and organising), Corporate Social Responsibility and sustainability initiatives (including pro bono work), sports, becoming a school governor and providing school support (such as reading groups).

» There is a committee or group for most things. If no group exists for your interest or passion, look to set one up, demonstrating your leadership skills and enhancing relationships with your colleagues.

SEAT 3: CORPORATE

'THE SHOW MUST GO ON'

In which Alex tries something new, solves some problems and sees the light at the end of the tunnel.

Alex sat and stared at her screen. The office lights were too bright. Unpacking was complete, but still papers cascaded along the right side of her desk, spilling into a box of confidential recycling at her feet. Running through her mind all at once: the thrill of the new, a tightness at the thought of meeting a new team, and apprehension at, once again, stepping into the unknown. She'd survived the mistakes of her second seat and the personal drama of the first. Now, after what felt like only moments, she's readying herself for seat three – corporate. She needed coffee.

Locking her screen, clicking on the little neon clock to show she'd stopped working on Project Moon, she pushed back her chair. The open plan office, and the chest-level divide meant she only had to stand to ask Chris, now in his fourth seat, whether he wanted to join her.

'Outside?', she asked. She waited until they were through the double fire doors and the lift button pressed before launching into, 'I can't believe we've changed seats already!'

'Tell me about it. Over a year in. The whole thing seems to be going so fast.'

'I know. I'd just got the hang of how the planning lot filed their stuff – let alone know anything about the work! Moving on seems crazy. How am I supposed to get my head around another new area?'

Chris chuckled. 'I completely get it. Do you have any ideas about qualification yet? That'll be the next decision – I have to choose something by the end of this month: four weeks in corporate and I'll have to decide whether or not I want to qualify here! I know a couple of people who qualified into their fourth seat but have no idea how they established they had any aptitude for it so quickly.' He pulled a face.

'I have literally no idea. Dan was telling me such awful things about corporate… Pulling documents together and up for 48 hours straight. That sort of thing.'

Chris just raised an eyebrow – they were about to find out.

'I haven't even thought as far as the fourth seat yet,' Alex went on, 'maybe a secondment, if I can get one? I really like the idea of seeing what it's like in-house or even at another firm. This is all I know, and I'd like something to compare it to!'

'It means you'll be out of the firm during the job hunt though. Not sure if that matters, but I deliberately stayed put so I can do a bit of internal networking.' He paused. 'Don't know if that was right or wrong, but I'm going to start emailing people about coffees – can't hurt right?'

From the lift they walked through the client reception, nodding to the front of house team in their matching uniforms and out into the late September sun. Chris looked back, conspiratorially, waiting for the doors to slide shut.

'I wouldn't listen to a word Dan says. I've heard a couple of times that he's cocked things up. He told all the current corporate trainees that he'd been put in charge of monitoring their work and dragged them into meetings to report to him! A load of crap!'

'No way. Really?'

'Honestly. Very odd. I actually really like what I've heard of corporate. Apparently, they involve you really quickly in the work – lots of it is notes of meetings, drafts of emails and letters, things like that. Common sense stuff that you can take a crack at. Even if there is some photocopying though – or, worst, managing a data site – at least it's a bit of a break from thinking!'

'A data site?'

'It's just cloud storage for information about a business; someone has

SEAT 3: CORPORATE

to log on and review it all. Not setting the world alight, but I guess we're responsible for setting it up and granting access to it, and it's good to feel you're contributing pretty quickly. I wonder whether AI will be able to do most of that by the end of the seat…?'

Alex thinks, as they edge their way through the late breakfast crowd.

'Ok, interesting. I guess I should give this some thought. I'll still miss the property team though – I feel like I'm only just getting to know them.' Then, to the barista, 'Flat white, please.'

* * *

Back at her desk and it was time to meet Sanjay, her new supervisor. A hugely successful corporate 'rain-maker' with a fearsome reputation, he'd only recently returned to the partnership from an extended sabbatical and so the trainee grapevine was distinctly lacking in detail on his treatment of trainees. He always wore braces, she knew that. Red ones. Old school. But that was about all.

'Angela, great to meet you,' as he swept into the room.

'Um,' a slight quaver, 'it's Alex.'

'Ok – well good to meet you, Alex; we have much to do! Pull up a chair.'

They spoke for 45 minutes and it was the best start Alex could have imagined. Two more references to 'Angela' aside – clearly that was going to be a war rather than a battle – Sanjay explained exactly what he wanted from her *and for her* over the coming six months. There were several large deals where she could immediately assist with production of ancils (ancillary documents, like board minutes) – the lead senior associate would fill her in. Where she would be working directly with Sanjay was on the 'General Counsel Conference', which would take up much of their time for the next six months.

'It's my brainchild,' Sanjay cheerfully confided, leaning towards her over the desk. 'Nothing earth shattering, but I have a feeling it could become a regular thing if all goes well. And *you* are going to be central to it. I need a project manager: someone to write lists, check them twice, check them a third time. Arrange speakers. Make table charts. Liaise with the PSLs. We're going to have a hundred people here from our leading clients. The GCC means all those senior lawyers that directly instruct us will be there – it's a hell of a networking opportunity. Think you're up to it? I really need your buy-in for this. It's going to be a team of two.'

Alex was silent for a moment. This was the first time anyone had encouraged her to participate rather than just giving her an instruction. Ok, it was rhetorical – she wasn't going to say no! – but there was something in Sanjay's earnestness that suggested he really did want her to be enthusiastic about the project. A first bond of trust.

'I'd love to get involved; seriously, it sounds great.' And she meant it – something completely different from the purely legal work she'd had so far. This would require forensic organisation, but she could already see it would mean getting to meet so many people from all over the firm in the event's planning.

'Good – we'll start today and get you up to speed with the work done so far. Could you put a weekly meeting in the diary; probably up that to twice a week as we get a bit nearer to the day itself. Just for an update; 'state of the nation' sort of thing. It's the keynote speaker and finalising the chair for each session that will be the priority – some of the PSLs are already looking into the various sessions, I'll send on the details.' The words came tumbling out; Alex wished she'd had her notebook at the ready, something she swore she would always have to hand going forward.

Sanjay swung back to his computer, thought better of it and turned back.

'I know this is probably a bit different from the stuff you've done in training so far, but you should know two things. First, corporate is 90% project management anyway. In the US we're known as 'transaction lawyers' – yes it's about getting the law right, but more than that, it's about guiding the process, pushing it forward. So this is a key skill you'll be demonstrating. Second, if we get this right it will be a great day – we'll raise the firm's profile and it will be fun, I promise. That's what we're aiming for. Go to it!'

Despite the PSLs also calling her 'Angela' for a few weeks – not their fault, rather a miscommunication on an email, long deleted but whose effects rippled far wider and longer than she would have liked – Alex really took to working with them. Many meetings were scheduled to determine the speakers, the break-out sessions for discussion, timings, and invitees, with the programme coming together quickly. A couple of topical discussion panels, a couple of workshops and four best-practice advisory sessions made up two streams of the one-day conference, bookended by a sincere welcome and close, to be extemporised by Sanjay.

Alex revelled in the creative nature of the project, the thrill of putting something together from blank pages. Just as she'd hoped, she was meeting people from a different world at the firm – liaising with the communications/AV team to work out a plan for the meeting rooms they were to use; talking to catering to make sure the delegates would be well fed; meeting the senior partner to brief her on what was proposed, Sanjay arriving at the end to compliment her on her good work (a moment to treasure) and to discuss the keynote speaker, yet to be determined.

'You love this, don't you!?' Carla teased one evening in the canteen.

'It's going so well!' Alex gushed, then, catching herself, 'I don't mean that I'm nailing it, I just mean I'm really enjoying it – it seems less like work, does that make sense? The days disappear.'

'I'll take your word for it.' Carla, struggling with a particularly uncommunicative supervisor and an impenetrable trust dispute that had pre-dated her arrival by two years and seemed likely to outlast her career, was already moving towards the array of sweets for those working late.

* * *

Two days later, midnight, and much of the enthusiasm had evaporated. Sanjay had left at six, as usual. He was courteous as ever and 'hoped' Alex wouldn't need to stay later to deal with his work; they both knew she would. She couldn't help but feel a little bit aggrieved – she was doing work directly for him, after all – but she understood that their roles were separate and rightly or wrongly, much of the admin sat with her. He had said on several occasions that she was doing well and, although a formal appraisal was yet to happen, it felt as though she'd really found her niche.

For tonight, the programme now sorted, it was time to send out copies together with formal invitations. Although they were going out by email, it had been agreed that the strikingly designed schedule really needed to be seen: its photo-quality paper and textured cover would create more of an impression in the hand than on the screen. Whether this was environmentally friendly was beyond Alex's pay grade; what wasn't, was sending them out. And so, she found herself stuffing envelopes, printing cover letters, stamping them with Sanjay's signature and stacking them ready to go out with the morning's post.

It wasn't too bad. The office was quiet at this time, the only company being two other people on the floor completing a deal that was, no doubt, going to run even deeper into the night. The office lights, on timers, had largely given up and the ferocious glare of the sole remaining LED in the vestibule by the printer hurt her eyes. She turned it off – the residual glow from the corridor and the green flashes from the machine (I have power!) gave her enough to see by. She even had some music on.

She hadn't imagined this bit of being a trainee. The whirr of the printer, the music, the low lights, the repetition of creating the invitation packs, was relaxing. She sealed the last envelope and sat back against the door to the stationery cupboard, satisfied. 'I'll take a moment,' she thought, 'listen to the end of the song then I'll ask security to order a taxi.'

That's where her PA found her at 7.30am.

'All ok Alex? Are these for the post?' Not even a flicker of surprise.

'Um, yes, thanks. I'm just going to pop home for a shower.'

* * *

Two months later. Alex had settled into corporate life. She gets to work on transactions with a number of the associates in the department. Most of the work is interesting. There are bits of complex drafting that have her hunched over her desk working and reworking a stubborn text which, however many times she looks at it, won't do what it's supposed to do. When she thinks it does, she takes it to someone senior and a red-penned version inevitably comes back, indicating changes. A couple of low-key corporate governance matters for big-name clients; a life-changing business sale for an owner of a local manufacturer, who having built up a business over 45 years is now selling to a private equity house.

The conference progresses: the calm before the storm, Sanjay calls it, as they wait for responses and confirm the various speakers. Alex's only current task is to keep a log of who has said they will come. Most of the responses have been positive. Some replies indicate that the original addressee has moved on to another job (within the client or elsewhere), and she duly passes this information on to the relevant client partner and other seniors involved with that client. In most cases they already know, but Alex has been with the firm long enough now to know that it's critical to demonstrate attention to clients and changes of personnel is one of those things that can catch you out at a meeting – the right hand must talk to the left, as Sanjay put it.

But there was a difficulty today.

'People are unreliable!' Sanjay fumed (as much as he ever did) as he stormed into the office they shared. 'We've lost the Director.'

The Director was his pet name for the keynote speaker: a career diplomat, a friend of Sanjay's, and referred to as the Director ever since a very long call some years ago where the Director absolutely insisted on being made director of a particular entity which, it turned out, didn't exist. His speech was going to set the tone for the whole conference – it had proved impossible to avoid the situation in the US and his discussion of inter-jurisdictional politics was going to kick start everything.

'Back to the drawing board.'

Sanjay had always encouraged her to speak her mind and when Alex found herself ready with a suggestion, she volunteered it immediately. She did so now.

'I've been working with the regulatory team a lot on that reorganisation project, Project Moon…' This was also one of Sanjay's, although run

BEING A TRAINEE SOLICITOR

out of another team. 'They seem to have a pretty good working relationship with the regulator and the deal's supposed to finish at the end of the week – unlikely, I know, but it should be done *fairly* soon. That might be a bit of an incentive to come and talk about policy.'

'Perhaps that'll finish by Christmas!' Sanjay chortled happily. 'But keep up the good work of course.' He twirled a pen, thinking. 'That's not a bad idea though, I'll talk to a couple of the other partners about it. Appreciate it.'

* * *

The day before the conference. A month left of Alex's third seat. Three things are on her mind.

One, where to go next: she still liked the idea of a secondment, although she had reservations about the lack of choice. You go where the firm sends you and that might be to a random desk, if it's a virtual secondment to a client. Also, she'd heard rumours about the internal networking that people do during seat four, trying to engineer their qualification into a particular department. Did she want to risk being away for six months, out of sight and out of mind?

Two, her suggestion that the keynote speaker come from the regulator had worked out. Now the day had (almost) come, she was looking forward to catching up with some of the wider team she'd been working with on Project Moon. She felt she was bringing people together.

Three, and most pressing, where the hell was the material from the external printer?

They'd chosen the same printer they'd used for the invitations, where everything had gone smoothly. Wandering round the conference suite, booked and ready for set up, she thought about the work that it had taken to get here – the lists, the spreadsheets, the endless loading of PowerPoint presentations. The final task was to put together the packs of materials for the day – copies of slides, complementary copies of books, a branded pen and notebook – and time was running out.

Then a call, and a sigh: the printers, guaranteeing delivery for 7am the next day 'as agreed' (it certainly was not). There followed some concerted negotiation which resulted in a promise to deliver at 5am but that was the best they could do. With some resignation, Alex headed for home having booked her 4am taxi.

* * *

'How do you feel?' Sanjay, relaxing with a glass of wine, feet up on a chair, the detritus of the conference around them.

'Exhausted. I was up at 3.' She smiled. 'I have honestly really really enjoyed it – one of the best things I've done so far at the firm.'

'Why, do you think?' There was occasionally an air of the psychiatrist with Sanjay – he liked you to investigate your own feelings, find your own answers. Alex really enjoyed working with him and perhaps most of that was the level of trust he offered. He let you make mistakes and let you fix them, but you never felt unsupported. She'd enjoyed the seat because she had been in control, because she'd been given responsibility, because she'd been able to meet and engage with people beyond two or three associates in the same department, because the big project had been successful and she'd contributed, because the work had been varied. She paused and considered how to summarise.

'Because I feel like I fit.'

Sanjay nodded thoughtfully.

'So, what next? You've had an excellent five months here although I know you still have work to do. I'd really like to see you qualify here. There are interviews, of course, and I can't guarantee anything, but I'd certainly support an application.'

Alex could feel her mouth switching, the start of a smile when you don't want to look too pleased but can't hold it in.

'I think that's what I want, and I really appreciate it. I'm hoping to go on secondment next so my qualification choices are going to be between the three seats I've already had. I'm pretty sure this is the right option for me.'

'Funnily enough, I also wanted to talk to you about that. One of the delegates today suggested that we spend a bit of time strengthening the relationship and actually proposed an exchange – one of ours for one of their internal legal team. It's got your name all over it. I could mention it to HR if you'd like.'

Alex started to speak.

'Hang on a sec – it's in Norway.'

***

'Do it!' Chris and Carla together.

'Honestly,' Chris went on, 'you'll regret it if you don't. It's such a lovely country and what an amazing opportunity.'

Carla nodded.

'I guess,' Alex sipping cold brew coffee. 'I just want to make sure that I'm not choosing the wrong time to walk away from the firm. How does qualification work anyway – do I need to fight a corner?'

'Absolutely not.' Carla this time, and the expert having qualified six months before. 'It's such a bugbear of mine. My view is that they've seen what we can do and they have interviews for internal jobs. They don't need anything more than that and trying to mount some sort of campaign just looks really desperate. Go for a coffee, fine, especially if that's suggested by someone in the department, but you don't need to. And it's six months in Norway – do it!'

Alex knew she was right. It would be refreshing to be away, to see how other people work. She had support in Sanjay and had found her space. With that platform it must surely be the time to spread her wings.

'You'll email me, right? Keep me updated?'

They shared a smile.

'Personal emails only!'

PART 3: COMPLETION AND BEYOND

12 | QUALIFICATION

You've come so far – 20 months in (let's say) – and it will be time to consider qualification. This is a big decision, something that will determine the initial direction of your career, possibly its entire trajectory. It's exciting, but it can be overwhelming. It can be tricky to work out what you've enjoyed and tie that into your future. Add to this the need to make choices fairly early in your final seat, while still finding your feet and wondering whether this could be the area for you, and it's not surprising if your head starts to spin.

Think about the present

The crucial thing is to make the decision for you. This must be the present you, not an anticipated future you, and certainly not looking as far ahead as partnership. Much will happen in the intervening ten or so years, professionally and personally, so the question is: what interests you right now? Which area(s) of law have you most enjoyed?

A follow up question: in which area or areas of law can you see yourself really developing? You may need to use your imagination for this second question as it will depend to some extent on the experiences of your seats and the extent to which you were able to get a holistic view of each practice area, but essentially is there a *style of practice* that appeals to you? Perhaps you really enjoy mastering complex legislation, so can see yourself maturing into a tax lawyer. Perhaps you love attending networking events and can see yourself as a 'rain-maker' in a corporate team? The area that gives you affirmative answers to these questions (or similar) is likely to be a pretty good choice.

I strongly advise against allowing the composition of the team to influence you too much; don't choose to qualify somewhere because you liked your colleagues, however hilarious the weekly meeting and despite the generous and deep pockets of a particular partner at Friday evening socials. Of course it will be a factor, that's human nature, but it shouldn't be a deciding one. The day after you join the team half (or more!) of them could disappear, poached by a rival firm or simply following opportunities elsewhere. A happy team culture is likely to continue, contentedness replicating in newcomers, and no doubt that will be part of your decision-making process. It will also, I'm sure, contribute to your initial attraction to a particular area of law – after all, working with good people is going to make the work easier and more satisfying. Yet your career is yours alone: what would you want to do if the individuals in those teams weren't there?

As a final thought, and despite saying that you shouldn't think too far ahead, do consider what your choice of practice area may mean for the future. A generalist field like commercial, corporate or property may facilitate moving from private practice to an in-house role should you choose to at some later date. Similarly, tax, regulatory or financial services roles may permit movements to consultancy firms or regulators. This is a factor to consider, but it should be (I suggest) a peripheral thought and not one to guide you.

Once qualified, if you want to try something else and you are passionate about it, you will find the right role. In-house lawyers are themselves talented generalists and multi-taskers (as you will know if you're training in-house) and you won't be severely limited by the choice you make now.

Process

The process can be opaque. Some firms require an interview, others don't. Release of the list of available jobs and, much later, the list of successful applicants can be arbitrary and poorly advertised internally. The process and its management is often dictated by the size and type of the firm.

For a cohort undergoing a typical two-year training contract at a mid-sized commercial firm and upwards (in size), the usual process is as follows.

Around four months before the end of a cohort's training a list of

12 | QUALIFICATION

available jobs will be posted. These are informed by the needs of the business, with each department having made a business case for additional junior resource. Although seniors won't make you any promises, especially where such decisions are made centrally, if you have stayed in touch (and we will discuss this further below) and communication is working well, you should have a good idea of whether a job is available in your chosen area(s).

Following issue of the 'jobs list' you will discuss the job you wish to apply for with your contact in the relevant department. It is at this point that it *does* become sensible to suggest a coffee and to talk through your application with that contact.

When you've made clear your interest, it is often the case that your former supervisor or another representative (the head of the department, for example) will contact you and arrange just such a catch up. The goal is to agree that an application will be welcome. If it won't be welcome, you're likely to have picked up on that feeling long before and wouldn't be looking to apply to that team. However, and unfortunately, people do get their wires crossed and it may be that you face being let down (hopefully) gently. At least you know at this early stage and can concentrate your efforts elsewhere.

Once you've established informally that the application is welcome, you formally apply for the job, usually through a centralised system. Quite what such an application looks like varies wildly between firms, from a common application form to a simple emailed expression of interest.

A month pre-qualification you will be invited to interview. This can be difficult, even awkward as it's likely to be with people you've previously worked with. A combination of feeling they already know what you've done, your capabilities, and the need for some formality in an interview setting may make this uncomfortable. It shouldn't be. Some interviews are an excuse for reminiscing about work done previously, others include testing questions to see how you respond to and apply common concerns of the department to unfamiliar situations. It will depend on the interviewer and the approach of the team.

BEING A TRAINEE SOLICITOR

The point, really, is to assess how much of the subject-specific knowledge you retained and gauge your continued enthusiasm. And this is a sliding scale: if you went through the department in your first seat, you may have forgotten much of the detail yet still demonstrate an interest in the work; if you're applying to join the department where you are spending your final seat, the subject matter will be fresh but you will have very limited experience to talk about given the timings of the interview. It's a judgement call on how you react to pressure, your reasons for wanting to join the department, and the quality of the impact you had on the team.

It may be a competitive interview if there are two (or more) applications for a single job, it may not – although that should have no bearing on the substance of the interview. You will need to prepare carefully, if only to maintain your reputation for diligence.

Within a week or so of the interview you should know whether you have been successful.

Having said all of this, I can't promise that this summary – the timetable or the content – is in any way definitive. Law firms come in many shapes and sizes and how they deal with qualifying trainees differs between them. Some of the very big and very small firms are likely to simply accept trainees into the team they request – there is no need for an interview as they know you well and they have the capacity (or have planned the capacity) to accept you without further formality. As I have already suggested, the rigorousness of the interview will vary considerably even within a firm. The way in which your firm undertakes the process is something that should be made clear to you early on in your training; if it isn't, you should feel free to ask.

Remember, the retention of trainees is a published metric and something by which firms are judged. In most cases your firm will want you to stay. The process is designed to match your ambitions to the firm's. If they don't, it's at that point you need to look further afield.

Interview preparation

How can you prepare for an interview in this context?

12 | QUALIFICATION

You will be pleased to know that this is where the dreaded – but necessary – time recording comes into its own. You have access to your timesheets (you should be able to export from the system), so remind yourself of the matters you were involved with. The utility of this will depend on the quality of your narrative. However, it should be enough to jog your memory no matter how cursory your write-up. Doing this is, I suggest, much more helpful than trying to read up on the work of the department in the abstract.

Talk to some of the junior qualified lawyers: how were their interviews in style and substance? What were they asked and how did they prepare?

Make sure you're up to date with the activities of any key clients for the department – the trade press is a good place to start. Similarly, pay attention to the activities of the department, the overarching strategy of the firm, and how they interlink. Initiatives for both are often announced on the intranet in large firms.

So, for example, if the firm is focused on increasing its client base in the hospitality sector and you're applying to commercial property, there are likely to be some ongoing plans for the team to target hotel chains. What have they announced to the rest of the firm that you can bring up at the right moment? Interviewers will be looking for opinions; they want to see how you have developed as a lawyer. It's about reasoning to an answer and showing awareness of the context (commercial or otherwise) of the department's practice.

Always look at what's available in the wider market, outside of the firm, regardless of whether you're actively thinking of leaving. It may be that despite not wanting to move you are obliged to, either because there isn't a job in the department you want to join at your present firm or because other firms offer a different package or opportunity – departments with combined specialisms that would let you advise more widely, perhaps. This isn't disloyal and it isn't preparing to fail. It's a sensible thing to do when you're applying for any new job, which, whether it feels that way or not, is what you're doing.

Staying in touch

Let's take a closer look at the rather nebulous concept of 'staying in touch' in the period between leaving a department and making an application to join it.

Where you're interested in qualifying into a team, even if you only consider that team as one option of several, then it's generally encouraged to seek to stay in contact. How do we distinguish this from the 'don't bug senior people for coffees – it will do no good' rule given earlier in the book?

Well, for a start we are talking about consistency. You show your interest by asking to stay involved in the life of the department from the point you leave. Demanding coffee with the head of tax a week before interview decisions are made won't help and is likely to be brushed off. A gentle campaign of attending team events, asking to remain on (or be added to) update emails/news lists so that you can stay up to speed on legal developments in the area, and/or speaking regularly to your former supervisor over the course of the year before such decisions are made will work very well. It's not a campaign for a job, rather demonstration of a serious and long-term interest in the team and its area of work.

You may find this second nature or you may think it sounds terribly pushy. The good news is that quite often it's the team that pursues you, especially if you've made clear during the seat that the type of work is to your taste. In my teams I made a point of organising a handover dinner to say 'bon voyage' to outgoing trainees and 'welcome to the team' to those joining, a great opening to reconnect with those former trainees who'd shown interest in the department. There's nothing formal about it and whether it happens regularly or at all will depend on the culture of your firm and the relevant department. If nothing else, it's an opportunity to catch up over some food.

As ever, don't panic if this doesn't happen to you and, instead, take the advice above about gently staying in touch with the team under your own steam.

Perhaps this doesn't need to be said. After all, having been part of a team, you will have found colleagues of all levels to remain friendly with,

12 | QUALIFICATION

that person you look forward to approaching for a coffee or lunch. If no-one sufficiently senior presents themselves – you're probably looking for a senior associate or junior partner, someone who can speak up for you – then it's perfectly acceptable to email the head of the department and express your interest. Don't worry that it will look brazen. The key is to do this as far in advance of the search for jobs at the end of the training process as possible to avoid it looking like an afterthought and, of course, to be relaxed and respectful in your approach. 'I really enjoyed my time in the department and would like to stay in touch, perhaps with a view to applying for a role' is the tone, not 'I've been told I was an excellent trainee in your team and can't wait to qualify there. Let me know when I start'.

Much of this pre-supposes that you want to and have the chance to stay at the firm where you trained. For a whole host of reasons, this may not be the case: you may want to move to a different part of the country; perhaps you feel a team at another firm has a better reputation. In that situation, carrying out research into the offering of other firms will be important. The services of a professional recruiter may be useful. With their broad experience of different firms, they will be able to advise on the cultural fit for you and which firms might be amenable to your application. Be open to all opportunities and possibilities – recognising your future may be elsewhere is mature, not failure.

Qualification is both an end and a beginning. It is the culmination of a huge amount of effort on your part and the start of what, hopefully, will be a satisfying and fulfilling career. This should be a time of excitement. Think about it as *your* chance to choose, a moment to sit back and review your options before moving on to the next stage of your career in partnership with a particular firm. Enjoy having reached the stage where *you* are in a position to make that choice.

Takeaways
» If you enjoyed the seat, stay in touch with the team and show an interest in its work.

BEING A TRAINEE SOLICITOR

- » When it comes to making a choice, it's the here and now that matters (albeit with a nod towards the transferability of softer skills to future roles, potentially outside the firm).

- » Choose the work not the people.

- » Focus on what interests you and ignore the approach and opinions of others in your cohort, however well intentioned. Your career is yours alone.

- » Be informed by checking your application will be welcomed, looking at what other firms are offering (in terms of available jobs), and prepare for any interview as thoroughly as if you had never met your interviewers before.

13 | SECONDMENT

Law is a service industry. It is built around relationships. Following the changing patterns of working that we've seen in recent years, post-Covid, we have become adept at creating relationships at a distance. Still, it is hard to better being in and around an organisation to understand what it does, its key concerns and the characters working within it.

For this reason, one of the ways in which professional services firms, particularly law firms, have taken to building relationships is by way of a secondment – a period in a different office, jurisdiction or with a client. This is prime territory for junior lawyers who are generally (not always) able to be more flexible in their location.

Firms that offer secondments as part of a training scheme almost always do so for the final seat. This arrangement gives you as much experience with business-as-usual work as possible through the early stages of your traineeship; secondments generally being seen as enhancing your soft skills in (as we've seen) relationship building rather than your legal or business skills. The secondment is most likely to take place either in a jurisdiction in which you don't practice or as part of a client team, and in either case is work that you wouldn't do as part of your day job at the firm.

Types of secondment

As part of the service firms offer, clients sometimes ask for a dedicated resource for a particular project or simply to support an internal legal team. This is often granted as a 'sweetener' to the client-firm relationship, an investment in its future. When a lawyer employed by a law firm dedicates all or part of their working time to a particular client, this is known as a client secondment. This might involve the seconded lawyer moving their place of work to the client's offices, or it could operate virtually whereby the lawyer continues to work in the firm but supporting only that client.

Some firms offer international secondments either within the firm, where it has a presence in multiple jurisdictions, or to other law firms. The offer of a secondment abroad is an incentive to trainee recruitment, a way of encouraging relationship building between international colleagues, and provides additional flexibility for short-term staffing in the context of the international business. Some firms have a network of linked/referral firms across the globe and maintaining links with and between these firms is a crucial part of that strategy. Sending people to work closely with lawyers in these partner firms results in strong personal relationships and, so the theory goes, a continuation of the network into the next generation of lawyers.

Where trainees fit into these schemes depends on the firm. In some, being seconded is seen as a reward for loyalty or a way of assuring someone that they are valued and have a future with the organisation. After all, there's little point sending your employees to work closely with a client or friendly law firm, developing contacts, only for them not to be given a job or choosing to leave, taking those relationships with them (although of course this happens).

For other firms, trainees are the obvious choice. Their time on secondment is necessarily limited (to the length of the seat); they are unlikely to be poached (at least, the risk is vastly less than it would be for someone more senior, with experience and contacts that are difficult to replace); and, much more positively, it is great experience for those trainees.

Reasons to consider it

If you are asked to go on secondment or you're able to put yourself forward for the opportunity, I encourage you to give it serious consideration. Let me explain why.

Generally – and I am *really* generalising here – junior lawyers aren't in charge of their own destiny. They support the rest of the team and client relationships are held by others. On secondment, your work will play out differently. You are likely to have greater responsibility. Outside the hierarchy of a law firm, or in a firm that isn't your employer, you will have the chance to spread your wings. You can use this freedom to explore your interests, with greater control over the projects you take on. You will have direct client contact, either the business of the client you're supporting or the clients of the law firm to which you are seconded. Lawyers at that firm will want you to become involved – you embody its international credentials and reach.

In a different business, you'll encounter new ways of working. For example, in a large manufacturing business the in-house legal team may play much more of a compliance role than a facilitating role. By that I mean that the main role of the lawyers will be to police what comes before them, enquiring more deeply into the commercial terms. Why have these terms been proposed? Why is the business choosing to expand into a new territory, given the different regulatory environment? Have those regulatory issues been considered, thought through and risk assessed? You are often seeking to save the business from itself.

This is the opposite of private practice, where most of the time your task will be to work out how to carry out a client's request – managing risk, certainly, but generally finding a way to say 'yes, this is doable'.

Clearly this is more nuanced than I'm making it. Still, you can see that there is a broadly different role to be played in each case. This is all invaluable experience at the outset of your career.

Separately, taking on a secondment will raise your profile within the firm. By definition you are likely to be seconded to a key client of the firm, one whose annual spend with the firm is considerable or where there is some strategic importance to the relationship. The contacts you build with its employees and your newly acquired knowledge of its business will be irreplicable and therefore highly valued on your return. It is no guarantee of a job on qualification, but it is logical to suggest that you're in a good position going into qualification interviews if you have a personal connection with one of the firm's most important clients. And this needn't be limited to established clients. Good performance with a new or less well-established client may lead to further instructions, bringing its own recognition.

The same is true for secondments to a friendly law firm or to an international office. As we saw at the beginning of this chapter, the relationships built between offices are what this exercise is all about. They are valuable and valued.

Secondments that offer you the opportunity to go abroad or to a different city aren't for everyone – as we will consider further below – but if you are in a position to be adventurous and would like to get to know another part of the world, this can make a wonderful change (which, as we know, is as good as a rest). There can also be positive financial effects as you may receive a *per diem* – a daily gratuity to recognise you are away from your base location – or payment of part or all of your housing costs (again to recognise the relocation).

So, a secondment should be given genuine consideration: it can open new horizons, increase your profile, possibly lead to travel, and may help with your employability. However, as with any decision, you need to make sure you've thought deeply about the pros and the cons before moving forward. Much will depend on your personal situation and your experience of training when you are asked to make the decision. Let's consider, together, the key things you should bear in mind.

If you're heading to a client, you are straddling two roles: in-house counsel for the client and a representative of your firm. This has the potential to bring a level of pressure. You will be regarded as a specialist even though you don't necessarily have the background understanding of the client's business. You shouldn't be overly concerned about this.

For the period of the secondment you are, to all intents and purposes, part of the client and should be subsumed fully into the organisation. The point to bear in mind is simply that you are, ultimately, an employee of your firm and so you must maintain an exemplary professional demeanour. This becomes more important, not less so, and remains true whatever the employees of the client do.

There are also practical considerations. You need to ask yourself

13 | SECONDMENT

whether the secondment will lead to you missing out on the opportunity to experience a seat in an area of law of specific interest. This can be tricky.

As we've already seen, you may request a particular seat but there's no guarantee it will come your way. This needs to be weighed against the advantages of a secondment discussed above. Remember, you will be able to discuss any opportunity with the client partner responsible for the client in question, the graduate team who allocate seats and, if applicable, your HR team. Although there are advantages to you in taking on a secondment, it is also an important moment for the firm which has chosen you as its representative. You will have some bargaining power, and a full and frank discussion should ensue. Perhaps you can gain assurances that you will be permitted to get experience of (for example) tax law in the future if you accept the secondment arrangements? Be confident that there is an element of negotiation available here.

If the secondment will take you abroad, consider the implications for your personal life. Will the firm offer any support to cover rent or travel expenses? How often will you want to go home or to visit your base location? What other support will be available to you?

If the secondment is offered for the duration of your last seat – very likely – consider how this might impact on your job prospects. Although, as we discussed in Chapter 12, you would do well to ignore the hype that surrounds job applications, there *will* be people you want to speak to in making decisions. Being away from the firm will make that more difficult. Still, everyone at the firm has been through the jobs process before and previous supervisors will (or should be) very happy to find half an hour to discuss the availability of jobs and/or how you might approach an application.

In my view, the opportunity to go on secondment is hugely beneficial for your self-development and for your career. You will get to meet and learn from talented lawyers that work outside your firm and to develop working relationships and friendships which are likely to assist as you progress in your career. You will need to be sure, however, that the interruption to your training and the disruption to your personal life is acceptable to you and, most importantly, that you feel that you will not miss out on learning.

If in doubt, talk to people at your firm who have been on secondment previously. Ask why they did it and what they felt they gained from the experience. For many, I'm sure, the experience will have been overwhelmingly positive, bringing a realisation that you can give competent and constructive advice alone, dealing directly with clients, thinking under pressure, being involved in a business. Where cautionary tales emerge (perhaps being thrown in at the deep end without an understanding of the relevant business, feeling slightly divorced from the activities of the firm), you will have a chance to consider this information in light of your interests and career goals.

Whatever decision you make, it must be the best one for you. My suggestion is simply that if you are offered the opportunity of going on secondment you approach it with an open mind. You never know what you will learn, who you will meet and what doors it might open in the future.

Adventures in Scandinavia

I was fortunate enough to go on secondment in my final seat. At the time, I used a diary to try and capture the nerves and the excitement, the fear and anticipation of the unknown. Here are some early entries; perhaps it will generate the same for you, when the time comes. As secondments vary so hugely in terms of location and tasks, in including these diary entries I'm trying to recreate the initial excitement for you. I appreciate there isn't an awful lot of information about what I actually did. Take my word for it, the experience was life changing and all the advantages I mention above (relationship building, greater exposure to clients, finding my feet) manifested.

Part 1 – It begins...

It's Saturday, September the first, 4am. Something big is about to happen. I've got a suitcase and a hold-all that, combined, are heavier than me. They're strapped to my body meaning I can't breathe, but I've only got to make the 50 feet to the waiting car. Blood running to my face, sweat

13 | SECONDMENT

dripping, I shuffle the last few yards, throw the bags on the ground and stumble to a standstill in front of the waiting driver. He – unsuccessfully – hides a smile.

'There'll be some excess baggage on that,' he winks at me. 'If you could just put those in the boot – I'd help, but my arm...'

I make it to the plane without mishap. The steward takes the trouble to show me to my seat, with notes about the seat I'm sitting in being adjacent to an emergency exit and this means that no coats, bags etc. can be left on the floor. They're 'sure I already know this', but I don't – I have no idea.

'So, aren't ya glad we're next to the escape hatch buddy?'

The voice is booming and sounds North American. I think he's joking.

'I'm not sure I want the responsibility of trying to open the thing if we go down,' I say.

'God, I'm a captain myself and I definitely want to be by this. I don't want some idiot getting in my way. It's survival of the fittest, friend, and I wanna be the first out of here if we ditch!'

He's honest at least. Is he really a captain? It's just not the attitude I imagine they'd have.

'Hey, can I have some nuts...?' he bawls.

* * *

Flying into Stockholm is an experience not to be missed. The expanse of water breaks into large, graceful lakes lapping at the shores of hundreds of islands as we skim the archipelago. The sun is out, the sky clear and we're full of good vibes as we gallop off the plane and I head outside to find a taxi.

It's a pretty ride from Arlanda airport. A wide, quiet strip of motorway leads into the CBD and the civic centre of the city and then across several bridges to Gamla Stan – the mediaeval heart of town. Ordinarily.

Unfortunately, I arrive on a day when the whole of the downtown district including the waterfront has been closed for the annual marathon. Of course, the taxi drivers would know nothing about this – presumably information about it having been distributed 'only' months before – and so were highly vexed by the road closures.

Ishmail (my driver) and I get on well up to this point. A slightly inauspicious start – 'You've come at a rubbish time of year; it'll be snow, snow, snow until February. Do you speak Swedish? You should.' – melts into a warm spring friendship as he tells me about his relatives in Slough.

But it all changes when we hit the jam. 'F***!'; 'S**t!', he bellows, banging the steering wheel and cutting up car after car. The 'jam' consists of about 10 cars – slow, indisputably, but not even a traffic blip in UK terms.

'It's a set fare,' he wails. 'If it takes this long [20 minutes!] to get you there, I lose money.'

I sigh in reassuring sympathy.

Finding we can't get any closer to the booked apartment, we stop in a random cobbled street.

'I can go no further...'

I tip.

* * *

The next half an hour is a trial I won't bore you with. Dragging heavy bags up steep, narrow streets is not the suave entrance I wanted to make to a new life. Sweating and shattered, I sit on a collapsed bag and try to get my breath back.

As I take in the surroundings, I seem to have fallen on my feet. It may be tourist central – Stockholm branded pens and pencils, Swedish flags and, inexplicably, a stuffed and mounted fox, are all on sale in the small shops in the warren of mediaeval streets – but it is beautiful.

Five, six story buildings with clean, definite lines and small doors and windows randomly interposed are coloured different yellows, reds and browns. Each building, residential or not, seems to have a restaurant at its base, tablecloths with candles burnt down to the wick. Outside seating to take full advantage of the fading days of summer.

After a while, I'm able to continue struggling through a crowded square behind a large church, I check my phone looking for the address of the apartment the firm has booked. Finding a discreet door, next to yet another taxidermy shop (really!), I punch in a code and the heavy door swings open.

Sinking into the warm arms of the sofa, I take stock. For the next six months, I was home.

Part 2 – The First Two Weeks…

Sunday brings with it a bright, wintry sun and I set out to see what Stockholm has to offer. Clutching a guidebook with its invaluable map, I follow the hill down past the imposing royal palace to the water and along the front. There, on the right, is a rambling building (a whole block) which houses my new office. It's an intimidating moment, but exciting too, filled with possibilities for the next half a year: work to do, people to meet, new experiences all.

On the first Monday, like any first day, I wake up ridiculously early and have time on my hands to think about the day ahead. Go in confident, I think, no time to be a shrinking violet.

After a quick coffee in a friendly shop next to the firm's entrance, I push open a mediaeval-looking oak door to enter the rambling, red-brick building. I make my way to a plush reception and say I'm here to meet Åsa, my mentor. These are all the details I have, sent on an email the Friday before. I take a seat, as instructed.

My arrival seems to have been co-ordinated to fit with the new intake of lawyers. Fresh faces join me in reception; at first in ones and twos, then larger groups. With each new set of arrivals comes another round of introductions in Swedish until, when there are around 15 of us, I'm gratefully plucked from obscurity by Åsa. Curious eyes watch me being led away.

I discover I'm sitting with the capital markets team, where my English (it's thought) can be put to good use in proofing documents. My colleagues seem delightful. In fact, the whole introductory process is stress free. Everyone is amazingly welcoming; the team pops in to my gloriously (and unexpectedly) substantial office, one at a time, to say hello. Typically,

I immediately forget every name.

The building itself is an absolute warren, extended incrementally over a century as the firm expanded and now consisting of two huge 'houses' connected by an attic walkway. I'm constantly lost.

The younger associates take me out for lunch. A thoroughly entertaining bunch, they're only too pleased to introduce me to their city. I order the chicken and a coke and sit back to receive the ravioli placed smilingly in front of me. I'm slightly puzzled but, a stranger in a foreign town, assume things are done differently here. I sweep up my knife and fork and prepare to get stuck in, prevented only by one of my new friends laying a restraining hand on the fingers clutching my raised fork.

'Um, I think that's my ravioli…'

Just goes to show that not everything should be taken at face value.

* * *

It's funny how similar people are in the legal profession. Asking for the stationery cupboard provokes great enthusiasm, and we process three floors down to find a room full to bursting with packs of pens, pads and the uniquely Swedish binder – a hinged spine with curved rings which mean that even when full it can be opened like a book. Genius.

And with that comes the end of the first day. As ever with things that you're worried about, it came and went speedily and without a hitch. Indeed, the whole of the first week comes and goes in the same manner. Work consists of training, familiarisation and meetings with various people who may have work for me in the future…but not yet. I have plenty of time to meet new people, adapt to a new environment, learn my way around the building. In a blink of an eye, the week has disappeared.

On the second Monday, everything's much more familiar; it's amazing quite how quickly you acclimatise to new surroundings. The nerves have gone (somewhat) and I'm looking forward to getting to know the people I work with a little better.

In fact, it turns into quite a sociable week as it's the firm's welcome

13 | SECONDMENT

dinner and introductory lectures for all new employees. I'd been invited and eagerly agreed to go.

'The lectures will all be in Swedish, but you can meet some people,' I'm told.

Not sure that this would be a massively effective use of my time, I decide to skip the lectures and just go to the dinner which turns out to be an elegant buffet in the atrium library (as grand as it sounds). I get talking to two people from the Frankfurt and Malmö offices respectively. We're joined by a tall, rather serious looking partner who speaks in Swedish to our small group for a couple of minutes, until Carin, one of my new friends, points out graciously that I don't speak it. Switching immediately to English, he peers imperiously down at me.

'Did you understand any of that?'

Cheerfully, I confess that I didn't but was 'hoping to look attentive'.

'You shouldn't do that,' came the riposte. 'People will think you know what's going on. You did understand when I mentioned X and Y firm though?'

The firms mentioned are internationally known with easily recognisable names, even amidst a stream of Swedish, yet I'd heard nothing of the sort.

'I'm sorry, I didn't catch it,' I stammer, deciding that honesty is the best policy. Then, imparting a confidence, 'I rather switched off.'

He stares at me for a (long) moment and then, with an adjustment to his glasses, smiles and the conversation moves on. It transpires he's referring to the talk given to the new joiners before the dinner – the part I'd skipped.

A glass of wine later and we're getting on famously. Commenting on the tremendously high standard of English in Sweden and fortified, I decide to attempt a favourite anecdote.

'I once got an e-mail from the accounts department of a European law firm. It simply said – in reference to an as yet unpaid bill – 'Please give me a call so that we can sort s**t out.'.'

I smile winningly into the steely eyes of the (I now know to be very senior) partner. I audibly gulp. Then, suddenly the eyes crinkle and we're all laughing.

'Apparently the author had a broken arm and found it difficult to type,' I explain. I leave shortly after, having skated close enough to the edge for one night.

* * *

It's the weekend. I finally get the time to do some exploring. Jumping on a mini-ferry, I head for Skansen, described in Lonely Planet as 'the world's first open-air museum, founded in 1891…around 150 traditional houses (inhabited by staff in period costume) and other exhibits from all over Sweden occupy this attractive hilltop'.

Traditional houses are just the start. There are björns (bears), wolves (vargs), but unfortunately no wolverines – a shame because I want proof that such a Hollywood sounding animal exists.

In the afternoon, I'm caught in the ultimate Stockholm tourist trap: sightseeing by boat. I join a crowd at the rear, open to the air, the wind in my face and the sun on my back.

As the boat moves off, the on-board commentary operates to a familiar rhythm – 'on your right you'll see Gamla Stan, on your left Södermalm, on your right the Stadhuset where the Nobel banquet is held each year…'

With every 'right' and 'left' we (the tourists) roll, jog and throw ourselves to the appropriate side, ready for a photo. Completely out of sync with the gentle movement of the water we stagger and fight for room for a picture. A couple of elbows to my head are a small price to pay for stunning sunset photos to show to the family back at home.

'An escape from the office,' I type, and press send.

Further study

This is a useful point to mention another option open to you: further study as a break, either during your training contract or in the early part of your career. There are organisations that offer competitive scholarships

13 | SECONDMENT

for study abroad to solicitors whether in training or qualified (although for practical reasons they tend to target those early on in their career).

At the time of writing, there are at least two opportunities, one for solicitors and one for barristers: the HM Hubbard Law Scholarship and the Pegasus Scholarship Trust. Lots of universities will offer international students some form of scholarship opportunity on application, particularly in North America.

Many people discount out of hand the idea of taking a break from their career so early on, but it can be hugely rewarding – the adventure of a lifetime.

I took advantage of the scholarship system to study for a post-graduate degree in Canada, an experience that changed my life. Writing on all sorts of topics – my 'dinner party' paper being an examination of the role of transitional justice and the rule of law in the popular sci-fi series *Battlestar Galactica* – I was able to get involved with the politics and social life of the faculty via a Graduate Law Students' Society and had the opportunity to plan two instalments of an interdisciplinary conference based out of the legal department.

Meeting lawyers from all over the world, almost all of whom went back into practice, this was a networking experience like no other. Even now, almost 20 years later, I can pick up the phone to people all over western Europe, Australia, China, Canada and the US should I need overseas advice for a client. But more than that, living abroad gives you a feeling of connection with the place: I will always see Canada as an adoptive home.

I mention this in a chapter about secondments because it similarly expands your horizons and your network. As with secondments, taking time away from a career you have invested most of your adult life trying to earn may seem a like a terrible move and, on my part, poor advice. Most junior lawyers are focused on progression, learning as much as they can as quickly as they can, and there is absolutely nothing wrong with that. After all, the purpose of this book is to give you a head start on your training. But the legal path in its traditional state is a linear one and there are relatively few opportunities, once you have started, to change discipline or to try new things.

Taking advantage of scholarships directed at lawyers can provide a moment when, if you are so inclined, you are able to step outside that pre-defined path as very few of your peers will, differentiating yourself. As you become more senior, this will become very important. At some stage in your career you will know more about an area than other lawyers; have more contacts; become close to a particular client. These are the elements of competition for partnership. Yet, even at trainee stage, you can start to mark yourself out.

Some of you will relish taking an unorthodox approach to your career and your choices are as valid as anyone else's: no knowledge or experience is wasted and if further study appeals to you, I encourage you to explore the options available. At the same time, each of you will have different personal commitments and professional aims. Completing your training is a huge achievement and considering horizontal steps – especially something as dramatic as taking up an academic opportunity abroad – will not be for everyone.

The message is not that you must or should do something like this – very few people do – but that you should always keep an open mind. This is especially true in proceeding from one role to the next, from trainee to qualified solicitor. You will recall the exhortation at the outset of this book to curate your career; this is the type of mindset that will assist you in doing so.

Takeaways

» Law is a service industry, built around relationships. A secondment – a period spent in a different office, jurisdiction or with a client – provides you with alternative perspectives and the opportunity to expand your professional contacts, while the firm gains an additional link in its network.

» Secondments could be to an international office of your firm, a client of the firm (providing dedicated resource for a particular project or

13 | SECONDMENT

general support), or to a partner law firm.

» Where trainees fit into these schemes depends on the firm. It is, however, prime territory for trainees given the additional experience it offers, and the six-month seat model lends itself to the process.

» A secondment is likely to provide you with greater responsibility, additional (and direct) client contact, experience of new ways of working, and potentially enhance your future role in the firm. This is all invaluable experience at the outset of your career. However, consider the implications for your personal situation – if it isn't the right decision for you, for whatever reason, don't pursue it.

» Linked, you could consider further study abroad by way of career break. Meeting lawyers from all over the world, many of whom go back into practice, can be a networking opportunity like no other. Again, it must be right for you as *you* curate your career.

14 | THE FUTURE

Nothing stays the same and training as a solicitor is no exception. Collectively, we know that there have been fundamental changes to the primary method of qualification in the SQE. Beyond the practical requirements, however, you will face challenges that are new to the whole profession. There won't be a well worn path through these issues although best practices will slowly emerge. You, your cohort and colleagues will need to navigate at least some of this together.

There are specialists in legal crystal-ball-gazing, those who keep their ears to the ground and their fingers on the pulse (and insert any other applicable idiom). This chapter is less about trying to predict what will happen in the wider field of law, and more about addressing some of the foreseeable issues you will face during your training years. We will look at some of the rapidly developing topics exercising the profession: the impact of generative artificial intelligence (AI), an increased focus on ethics and the pandemic-legacy of hybrid working.

There will be others, only some of which are known at the point of writing, that emerge throughout your time as a trainee. All I want to do for now is give you a sense of the evolution of practice – it is in the nature of things that the profession you join won't remain the same for long.

The SQE: its pros and cons

The regulatory approach to training has undergone radical change with the SQE, and alternative routes to access the profession are already in place, including as a Chartered Legal Executive and via legal apprenticeships. As we have seen, the training contract is no longer strictly required, replaced with the obligation to carry out a period of recognised training

– currently still set at two years in aggregate – although most firms will continue to offer a formal contract and use the terminology.

Yet in many ways it is business as usual. The profession and its regulator both remain convinced that a period of on-the-job training is required before qualification, so the approach to training we have investigated and the skills you need to hone to get the most from that period will be the same. Many of the departures from the status quo are aimed – absolutely correctly, in my view – at inclusivity and access. If the period of recognised training doesn't have to be contiguous there should, in theory, be more scope for those without access to a formal training scheme to qualify into the profession. The often prohibitive cost of the LPC has been removed.

Some of the advice set out in this book will need to be adapted for your circumstances, should you take a non-traditional route. Apprentices, for example, will spend a much longer time as part of the firm, moving around less than trainees but with potentially much deeper experience. This means that qualification discussions will take on a different tone as you are part of the fabric of the organisation and the relevant team in a way that trainees are not. Whether that makes those conversations more or less difficult remains to be seen.

That said, the SQE has had a significant impact on all aspects of training. There is now the added pressure of exams to contend with while you're working. Trying to work and study at the same time, something that generally didn't happen with the LPC, has been deleterious to many would-be solicitors. Although we're still in the early days of the SQE, there are reports of trainees having to pause the course, or take time off from work, because of the exam pressures. Something will have to give, whether that is a period of paid leave (akin to the arrangements put in place to take the bar in the US) or a shake-up of the timings, such that the SQE is completed before or after training. Whatever happens, elevating the tension and making conclusion of the process of qualifying suddenly uncertain seems to be here to stay. Incomers to the profession will need to pace themselves; qualification is no longer a function of time served.

It is – in my view – more onerous, but there are advantages to the new

14 | THE FUTURE

approach. You find yourself in a professional environment more quickly and rather than paying lip service to skills training long before you reach a client, risking those skills becoming rusty, under the SQE system you will need to hone these skills at the moment you need them most: on the cusp of qualification.

The LPC has long been divisive in the profession, charging huge fees for a preparatory course that is, arguably, unnecessary. Apart from ensuring that some common professional jargon is understood, the content is necessarily limited because of the huge amount of ground the course was designed to cover: introductions to civil and criminal law, specialist electives, skills-based assessments, Solicitors Accounts Rules, professional conduct, the list goes on. Under the new system, you are instead able to focus on the type of work carried out by the firm that you intend to – or hope to – be part of. In short, a potentially stodgy year of generalisations can be focused into directly applicable lessons in the workplace at a faster pace.

I don't want to dwell for too much longer on the LPC and the SQE, given that almost all of you reading this will be on the SQE pathway – we are where we are. But it's worth a whistle-stop review of why the SQE was adopted.

I've already mentioned access and inclusion, important points both. The SRA's view was and remains that a final qualification exam has the dual benefit of ensuring 'high, consistent, professional standards' across the profession (as it was described in the October 2016 consultation paper which kick started the reforms), while allowing the approach to training to be modified without dilution of the ability of qualifying cohorts. The SQE also aligns with other common law countries – for example, New Zealand, Australia, Canada and the US (in the case of the latter three, managed on a state or province basis) – which all have a form of final qualification exam for their lawyers. This provides an objective measure to assess whether trainees have reached a standard appropriate for practice.

There is far from a consensus that the SQE will produce (or is producing) these high standards. Views have been expressed that reducing the process to a series of tests will give candidates an incentive to do the bare minimum to get through and qualify, with no regard to the depth of their training. It is for this reason that the SRA has repeatedly emphasised the importance of maintaining a period of training in the workplace.

The difficulty is that most firms, used as they are to the way a two-year training contract operates, are loathe to move away from it, whatever prior training you have done. This is fair enough. The two years of your training is about more than experiencing law and learning professional practice, as we have seen. It's about understanding how the firm operates, its concerns and values. Firms will (or are extremely likely to) want you to go through a programme they have designed. On that basis, although this is a brave new world, for many of you the training experience is unlikely to be any different to that of your antecedents.

After all, final set of exams or not, it is experience and empathy which will set you apart as a lawyer – your ability to understand a situation and work out how to deal with the people involved to improve or resolve it. There is no better training for that than being in the professional environment and soaking it up, seeing how seniors deal with clients, problems, others in the team. Far from reducing the work experience element of qualification to a formality, the new approach puts greater emphasis on good quality training (even if disaggregated). This is yet another reason to participate as fully as possible in any way that you can, in the life of the firm or firms you join.

Generative AI

Generative AI – technology that creates responses to user prompts for information or content – is already and will become increasingly important to all aspects of professional service. If you revisit the items listed as typical trainee tasks in Chapter 2, you will see that AI can assist in almost all of them: legal research and research notes, drafting emails, and researching clients (subject to the significant caveats below).

The speed at which the field of AI is developing means that a detailed treatment of its implications and uses here is redundant – it would be

14 | THE FUTURE

out of date as soon as this book is published. That said, there are general implications for you as current or future trainees that will remain the case no matter what happens with the technology.

The huge benefit for you is the doing away with the need to start with a blank page. Any piece of writing you've ever done – an essay, a report, an application – began with a blank page. A blank page which taunts you as you try desperately to work out where to start. The same was true when I first opened my laptop to begin this book. Structuring your thoughts to get something down on paper is the hardest part of any project. Generative AI can have a dramatic impact on this chilling effect, producing something in seconds for you to consider and review.

One of the many truly helpful things trainees bring to the firm (and those they work with) is production of a first draft. It is vastly easier for someone to sit there and review your work – however much it needs to change thereafter – than produce it themselves. It takes away that 'blank page' paralysis. Remember that, especially if somebody is criticising work you have done or where they are busy making wholesale changes in red pen.

The contribution of Generative AI is similar, although now it is providing that assistance to you, the trainee. You ask it a question and it will give you something to work with, whether that's legal research, information about a potential client, a draft of an email, or even a first cut of a legal document (your firm may or may not be using AI in that context). However – and this is the important thing – *that is all you should regard it as doing*. It is producing an unreliable text that gives you somewhere to start; you cannot expect AI (at least, at the time of writing) to give you any sort of instantly usable answer. It is a rough starting point only that needs to be checked, revised and refined. That's if it is used at all – it may be nonsense.

AI models generate content based on data fed to them. This is an exercise in statistics about which words are likely go with others. It isn't a 'human-like' intelligence, so it has no ethical compass or real understanding of what is being asked. Tales already circulate of arguments or citations being put forward based on material AI has simply made-up – so-called 'hallucinations'. In addition to doubts about its content, you can't accept at face value the way in which AI decides to structure its output. Once again, you need to treat it as somewhere to start which, ultimately, needs to be reconstructed as your work.

I don't want to sound unduly negative. AI is, without doubt, a powerful new tool which will benefit you tremendously. But it must be treated as any other tool; use it to produce a rough cut, fine, but the responsibility remains on you to ensure the final product does what is required and reflects your views.

Be prepared, also, for guidelines from your respective firms around the use of AI. It is not – or should not be – a free-for-all. The governance of AI i.e. the way it is used within an organisation, is an issue to which most organisations are hyper-alert, hyper-vigilant. This is because, unlike most strategic risks and opportunities organisations face, AI has the potential to 'creep' into all aspects of the business with very little encouragement. It isn't going to require a hard sell from senior management to get employees to start to use a tool that's regarded as such a time saver. Indeed, it may be adopted in parts of the business without management knowing.

For law firms, whose business is managing legal risk, the implications of AI are huge: there are copyright issues in the data given to the model; there are data protection and confidentiality issues in allowing AI access to the firm's data; there is a professional negligence risk in allowing lawyers to use AI for legal advice. It is for these reasons that the firm is likely to have a detailed policy on how, when, and in what context AI can be used. And there will be residual resistance to its use; generations of lawyers before you will have started with that blank piece of paper, why shouldn't you earn your stripes that way?

That is not the same as saying firms will be resistant. They won't. Every professional services organisation I am aware of has at the very least provided an integrated generative AI product as part of its available browser. AI is here and will be a big part of the future. Just remember that it is of limited value in terms of the final product. You will still be required to use all the skills previous generations of trainees needed: careful legal research, effective communication, conscientious project management and so on. Use the tool but treat it as such.

Ethics

One could make the argument that ethical decision making won't be something you'll have to worry about as a trainee. After all, the decision to take on a client, to act for them, almost certainly won't rest with you. The work that you do shouldn't, in theory, be imbued with ethical risk. But we're talking about something wider here, an increased emphasis on ethics throughout the profession following major scandals like that of the Post Office and its fallible software, where lawyers were front and centre in advising on what is now acknowledged to be a gross miscarriage of justice.

The Law Commission has published a consultation entitled *Upholding Professional Ethical Duties*, designed to ensure that the professional is resilient to the pressures of powerful vested interests which 'can test even the most principled practitioners, making it crucial that we create a working environment that supports and empowers ethical decision-making'. (See https://legalservicesboard.org.uk/wp-content/uploads/2025/03/PERL-Consultation-Document-February-2025.pdf).

The consultation sets out proposals for standards of professional ethics that the SRA, as our regulator, will be encouraged to pursue. In sum, there will need to be oversight of the extent to which we, as lawyers, have the right knowledge and skills about professional ethical duties, both at the point of qualification and throughout our career, set within an appropriate framework of rules and guidance. The emphasis on this being an ongoing duty means it will be something in which the regulator will continue to be interested.

How ethics should be taught and what standards should be upheld, and how that relates to your duty to your client, will therefore be a running theme for the near- to mid- future. This, combined with an increased emphasis on ESG and the sustainable and social elements of business, foreshadow some interesting conversations in your firms around which clients to take on.

And this need not be an issue of seniority. It involves questions of morality. At the time of writing, President Trump is taking action against certain US law firms, and some people at the junior end of those firms are starting to speak out publicly about whether their firms should be doing more to combat what they see as the damaging activities of the US administration.

Granted, it's unlikely that you will find yourself having to take a public stand in that way, but questions around the type of work being done by the firm and the kind of clients the firm acts for are going to become ever more prevalent.

Hybrid working

We discussed this at some length in Chapter 1. How might the newly available permutations of work develop for you in the future?

The trend is for organisations to start to draw lines setting out what the working week looks like to them, whether that's five days in the office, three days in the office, wholly remote options or any other variation. This will be an additional element for those of you entering the job market, legal or otherwise, to consider. Rather than location, location, location – to borrow a phrase – the decision facing you will be whether you want to be in the office at all.

This, of course, may indicate something deeper than a preferred working style.

A firm that permits you to set your own pattern of work might be seen as an organisation which trusts its staff. It might also be indicative of a very hands-off management style, and one with less of a distinctive culture by virtue of its (potential) lack of a buzzing office.

A firm which mandates full-time attendance in the office might be seen as less flexible when it comes to the preferences of its people, and more inclined to micro-manage. It could also be an organisation which values in-person contributions and interactions above all else, where the office is intentionally made a haven of creativity and play.

I'm not suggesting you can identify the culture of an organisation

14 | THE FUTURE

simply by its approach to remote or hybrid working. However, that approach will demonstrate more than preference or practicalities – it is part of that firm's approach to its workforce and will become part of your decision-making in choosing where to apply.

This will become increasingly important if, as appears to be the case, firms start to actively differentiate themselves through hybrid working. The difficulty – at least for now – is that this isn't true across the board. Stories abound of a disconnect between recruiting teams and their legal teams, where roles are advertised as remote or hybrid only for it to become clear that the legal team's expectations are that attendance is very regular.

It's also important to recognise in this context the potential impact on mental health. Many firms now have resources in place to help you if you're struggling, from mental health first-aiders to approach in a crisis, to mental health champions who take on the responsibility of planning initiatives to improve mental well-being across the firm. Working in isolation suits many people, some even prefer it. Others find it debilitating. It is important to recognise this and reflect on what works for you.

The good news is that you will always be welcomed into the office, so, if being alone at home makes you feel somewhat divorced from the life of the team, there's an easy solution. The tough part, perhaps, is to recognise your feelings. Always talk to someone you trust if things start to become too much.

Whatever else happens, hybrid working is the new normal. As I said at the very beginning of the book, it may not have occurred to you that the world of work could be any different. The flexibility of your working life is now far greater than at any time in the recent past, but it's not without its pressures. In many ways, heading into the office five days a week is reassuring in its predictable consistency. Any other model means rolling with things a little more. As with other pieces of advice in this book, the message is to reflect on what suits you – how, when, and where do you work best? As a trainee, you might not always have options, your presence in the office may be required. But that won't be all the time.

Takeaways

» You will face challenges that are new to the whole profession – indeed, to much of professional life.

» The regulatory approach to training has undergone radical change with the SQE, although most firms will still offer a formal training contract and will continue to use the terminology.

» The added pressure of exams to contend with while you're working means that incomers to the profession will need to pace themselves; qualification is no longer a function of time served.

» Generative AI is already a wonderful tool, likely to become central to your work. Ask it a question and it will give you something to work with, whether that's legal research, information about a potential client, a draft of an email, or even a first cut of a legal document (your firm may or may not be using AI in that context). However, that is *all you should regard it as doing*. It is a rough starting point that needs to be thoroughly checked, revised and refined (if used at all – it may be nonsense). It must be used in line with guidelines from your respective firms.

» Oversight of the extent to which we, as lawyers, have the right knowledge and skills about professional ethical duties will increase following well-publicised scandals. Questions (internal and external) around the type of advice provided and the types of clients firms act for are going to become ever more prevalent.

» Hybrid working is here to stay. A firm's stated policy will demonstrate more than preference or practicalities – it is part of that firm's approach to its workforce and therefore part of your decision-making about where to apply. Reflect on implications for your mental health. Some people find working in (physical) isolation difficult; others welcome it.

SEAT 4: SECONDMENT

'LEAVING TRAINING BEHIND'

In which Alex reaches the final hurdle, experiences work in a different environment, reflects on what she's accomplished and looks to the future.

'You leave at what time?!' Carla – incredulous – on the phone.

'The place is normally dead by 6, so that's probably the latest. I like to make sure most people have gone and there aren't any final questions. Everyone comes in pretty early though.'

'And there's no work to do in the evenings?'

'Nope. Not for me at the moment, anyway. That's why I'm calling you! And I wanted to know how everything's going, of course.'

Carla had qualified into the property team and Alex missed their regular catch ups over coffee. Working in-house was a completely different experience, and so far a really enjoyable one, but she rather missed being surrounded by the trials and tribulations of the other trainees.

Norway, unfortunately, had fallen through. 'We have to do more with less,' the email from HR read, 'and the same client is happy for you to do the secondment from its UK base in…High Wycombe.'

Ok, it would have been wonderful to spend six months discovering the delights of Oslo, scoffing pinnekjøtt and investigating hygge, but High Wycombe meant she could commute, and friends and family were as close as ever. To be honest she was just pleased to leave the firm: 'a change is as good as a rest' had never been more true. Most of her cohort had already started to talk about qualification and jobs options; she knew it was natural, but it seemed to be the focus of every conversation. Carla thought it amusing people got so worked up. In her time, she'd been known to announce at lunch that she'd lined up drinks with various heads of department to discuss qualifying. She hadn't, of course, but she liked to watch the ripple effect.

'I think I want to qualify into corporate,' she'd told Carla earlier on. 'Being serious – for a minute – do you think I should do anything about it?'

'Well, you could drop Sanjay a line and say that,' she replied thoughtfully, 'but didn't you have that discussion at your final appraisal?'

'Oh yeah, definitely. I said I was really interested and he said to keep in touch with the team. I only left, like, a month ago, but it seems ages.'

'Ha! But overall, it's flown by, right?'

'Insanely so.'

Carla laughed. 'We'll be partners before we know it. Drop him a line and just remind him that you're interested; it can't hurt.'

As it happened, the team reached out to her. One of the senior associates she'd worked with emailed to ask whether she could make it to the corporate team social to welcome their new trainees. 'It would be good to catch up,' the email read, 'especially with qualification decisions soon to be made.' Sanjay followed up more directly: 'Let's get a coffee in the diary and discuss jobs.'

***

Though the hours at the client were pleasing, the work was hard. Rather than just providing a sensible legal answer, Alex's role was general legal support and so she received questions about anything and everything. There was very little supervision: everyone was so busy that the overview role simply didn't exist. At first, she found it worrying that decisions were made and documents signed off on her say so, but a call with Danny about a piece of property work made her feel better.

'They're going to sign this anyway, Alex. Any sensible input you can give will improve matters. And this is excellent preparation for qualification – yes, there'll still be someone looking at your work when you come back to us, but you'll be expected to make decisions and drive projects without constant review. That freedom is part of the fun of moving up in

SEAT 4: SECONDMENT

the world. Incidentally, do you have time for a coffee to discuss jobs?'

Elated that the shredding of the original had clearly been forgotten, and feeling more empowered to deal with issues that cropped up, Alex settled into the rhythm of in-house life. She reviewed commercial contracts, opined on employment terms, agreed banking terms and, where the matter was too specialised, instructed lawyers.

'You've made quite an impression,' Danny told her over their coffee. 'We've had some terrible people go on secondment! One of them failed to find somewhere to live in time to begin, so slept in their car in the car park. Ironically, they got asked to leave after turning up late repeatedly. So, perhaps not a very high bar to do better than that. Anyway, have you thought about qualification?'

Danny took the news that Alex was focused mainly on a corporate role in her stride and said that she looked forward to working together soon; if Alex wanted to discuss interview tips she would be only too happy. Even Nathan had been in touch to wish her the best for the future, although his notable silence on that future being in commercial litigation spoke volumes. We are where we are, she figured.

In any event, qualification thoughts had to take a back seat. A major commercial contract had apparently been 'negotiated' between the engineering teams for eight or so months. Word of this reached the legal team with a week to go before (it was proposed) the project began. The first Alex knew of it was a call from a friend in the client's commercial team.

'Oh hi Alex, I wonder if we could meet quickly to talk through something. I've got a commercial matter that's due to sign next week. It's a pretty big one, it comes right from the top, but we thought best to run it past legal, just in case you have any comments.'

Alex sighed to herself. This happened all the time. No one would dream of signing anything that hadn't received legal approval, but a week was deemed sufficient for the most in-depth review. In practice, this meant the matter was delayed while either all the issues Alex would inevitably raise were dealt with or the business moved ahead anyway, taking a view on those issues which no one had the time or inclination to address.

BEING A TRAINEE SOLICITOR

After two meetings which everyone failed to attend, Alex finally got a copy of the proposed contract with a day to review and two to negotiate. She thought back to Sanjay's advice and got to work. Her issues list concentrated on the really bad: those points which she thought were legally inappropriate or incorrect or which seemed completely nonsensical from the client's perspective.

It took some courage. The expectation was that the project would be signed off. Alex knew such a list of concerns would mean considerable wringing of hands in order to get agreement to push the project while the position was considered (or, as she suspected would happen, the appropriate level of sign off was achieved even with the problems she'd identified). She sent the email and tried (and failed) not to worry about it overnight.

* * *

Her inbox the next day overflowed. There was some attempt to lay the blame at legal's door, but, overall, the response was supportive and the commercial team reluctantly accepted (she saw) that further work was needed. The timetable adjusted, Alex could breathe again.

It wasn't the end of the issue. A senior member of the commercial team walking past her desk, unexpectedly passed comment.

'That was a good email you sent yesterday – mature. Really helpful to have the risks pointed out along with some solutions, although I agree that we need to give this some more thought. Good to see some useful work from someone at your firm – you know we've had real problems with them in the past, right?'

Alex wasn't sure what to say. She'd heard of the issues with a former trainee, but didn't know the wider context of the relationship. She didn't want to make things worse, but to nod and accept it seemed disloyal.

'That's really kind,' she started. 'I don't know the background to the other stuff, but perhaps we could organise something between your team and the firm – maybe it'll help to put some of the past misunderstandings to bed? I've been meaning to set something up anyway. What do you think?'

SEAT 4: SECONDMENT

Alex faced similar diplomatic difficulties at the firm's Christmas party. The jobs list had been released and the corporate job Sanjay hinted at was duly present. The downside: at least two other people were applying. By some alchemy, everyone seemed to know who was applying where.

'It's everyone for themselves at this point,' Carla consoled her, 'and everyone has the right to apply.'

'Of course.' Alex nodded. 'I just don't want to disappoint someone, or be disappointed myself! It's so hard when we're all friends and we've been through this whole process together.'

'It's about being professional and mature, right? I guess that's why the interview process exists – in theory the right person gets the job, but I know it's a tense time. Anyway, let's dance and forget. A bit of right left, right left is just what this party needs.'

Yet the flashing lights of the dance floor must and did give way to the strip lighting of the interview room.

'Tell me,' one of the two corporate senior associates interviewing her asked, 'what's your personal business development approach?'

Alex's mind went blank – what on earth were they on about? Her voice was tight.

'Could you clarify the question?'

'How would you approach business development at your level? What's your plan?'

Knowing she didn't have one, Alex launched into an explanation of the proposed social between the corporate team and her secondment department.

'It's nothing special, just some drinks, but I think bringing the teams closer could really help.'

She remembered something Nathan had said to her during her first seat.

'It will be useful for me, building up my relationship with some of the juniors. After all, at this point it's all about getting to know the other professionals we'll age with! That way we'll have contacts when, as seniors, we'll need to bring work in.'

That got nods, but they were holding their cards close. As she left the room, she had no idea how it had gone. They'd asked quite a lot of questions about corporate law (as you might expect) but it was very hard to recall the detail now she'd left the seat, especially under pressure. She hoped she'd done herself justice; she was worried she hadn't.

***

'How did it go?' was the question in the canteen.

'No idea – you know how these things are. I kept talking. Anyway, finishing training is the main thing. I've been looking at other firms and there are other opportunities. I'll wait and see.'

From the corner booth snatches of conversations filtered through.

'Well, if I knew that, Mum, then we'd all be a bit calmer, wouldn't we?!' Silence. 'It's not that sort of thing.' A beat. The pitch increased. 'No, I can't follow up with an email saying how hard I work – it's a given!'

At least, Alex thought, things were a bit more relaxed for her. She hadn't mentioned it to anyone, but she'd been offered a job in-house at the client. They'd been very kind about the work she'd done, her independent approach and her interaction with the business. She knew she wanted to stay in private practice for now, but it took the pressure off to have a reserve. She'd been honest about her intentions. The corporate team had promised to respond by the end of the week and she hoped the job would be hers. She would wait and see.

What she knew for sure was that training had changed her. With six weeks to go, the end in sight, she finally had some perspective. It was more than development as a lawyer, learning to operate in different areas of law, learning to advise. She'd made mistakes, and solved them. She'd clashed with a colleague, and come to an accommodation. She'd volunteered, met new people and tried new things. She'd learnt to make decisions alone, where needed, and worked in a team on most days. She'd accepted that other people would go down a different path and that her career was bespoke. She'd made friends throughout the firm. She'd faced pressure, survived, and, she realised, enjoyed herself. It was time to move on to the next stage.

She was ready.

15 | FINAL THOUGHTS

The trainee considered the question, chewing contemplatively.

'It'd be nice to have something with a bit of guidance in, you know? Nothing too heavy. Something to think about. Give some signposts. I mean, I wouldn't say I didn't have a clue, but I certainly didn't know much!'

Back in the pub, sipping coffee with the early morning drinkers, I too had little idea how to approach training. It was my first day as a professional, my first real engagement with the practice of law, my inaugural office job. This book is an attempt to give you some advance flavour of what awaits during training, a roadmap for your training years. It is necessarily general. Your experiences will differ immediately, the areas of law you engage with and your ambitions diverging on day one. Still, there is value in *imagining* what training will be like, in anticipating what you might find challenging or, just as important, enjoyable and how you might deal with those experiences.

Together, we have considered the role of a supervisor and how to create a working relationship which benefits both of you; we've also seen how you might approach situations with a recalcitrant, unwilling or unavailable supervisor and how you can overcome that hurdle. We've discussed how to work with others, maintaining a cheerful approach to working while taking care to be accommodating to the ways of working of others and reflecting on your approach to the job.

We've looked at the structure of the training – and points of change in the near future. We've briefly examined the different frontline roles in a typical law firm and the way in which legal services are offered as a business proposition. We've looked at the chequered flag: the approach to and choices involved in qualification.

And we've seen some of this in practice through the eyes of our friend and fellow trainee, Alex.

Training, and subsequently qualifying, is a profound experience which is more than simply a route into the profession. During these years you are setting the foundations for the lawyer you will be. You will pick up habits, mostly good, that you will carry with you throughout your career. As with any sort of training, what you get out will depend on what you put in and I encourage you to take every opportunity that comes your way, from getting involved in CSR initiatives, attending and creating social events and spaces, volunteering your burgeoning legal skills to progress pro bono initiatives and generally leaning in.

At the same time, it's important to remember that this is a learning experience for you. The point of this book is not to try to make you an expert before you join a firm or to suggest you take on more than you can handle. You are new to the profession, perhaps new to the workplace, and this is your time to soak up knowledge and experience. So, ask questions all the time, ask for help if you need it, take advantage of the mentorships that are available to you (a mentor is a good supervisor by another name).

At the end of two years (or whatever period, in the future, is deemed sufficient for qualification), when you look back at your Day One self you will be amazed at your development in character and ability. When I broached the possibility of this book with trainees in my practice I asked them: 'What do you know now that you would tell your Day One self to make the experience better?' The universal response was 'have confidence'.

This meant something slightly different to each person – have faith you can do the work, have the belief that you are as good as others in your cohort, be more comfortable public speaking, be better at speaking up and asking for help, be more friendly, be more involved – but the commonality is clear. It is a big step, but nowhere near as hard as it might seem.

That answer – have confidence – demonstrated how much they had grown through the process. They would choose to tell their earlier incarnations that they could do it, that they were up to the challenge because, by the time I spoke to them *they were*. They had accomplished what they

15 | FINAL THOUGHTS

set out to do and survived and thrived in a training situation.

We can't teach confidence in the job, and we shouldn't. You will learn as you go, and you won't (and can't) know everything when you start. That is life. That is experience.

What we can do, and what this book has tried to offer, is provide you with a description of training, its structure, potential pitfalls and suggestions for making the most of it. Not as a blueprint, but a taster of what's to come, giving you a different kind of confidence: confidence that you know what you're signing up to. Understanding what is likely to be required of you and the active role you can play in preparing for that role means that you have already accomplished an important first stage of being a lawyer: reflecting on your strengths and weaknesses and being prepared to learn.

This is a practical guide to going about training as a solicitor, something more than simply learning to do a job. It is a flexible and encouraging system which permits you to explore your future style of working – in law, with people – with a safety net of the input and oversight of professionals who really do care about the next generation. Your story will be unique and special, and you have as much control over it as your firm and seniors. Perhaps that is the ultimate ambition of this book: to encourage you to hit the ground running in building your career. I wish you all every success.

GLOSSARY

Some of the less obvious terms used by practising lawyers. This list makes no pretension to be exhaustive but picks up some of the more commonly used words, phrases and acronyms which have the potential to cause confusion. It is, I'm afraid, heavily weighted towards commercial law firms.

All parties meeting/call: As it sounds, this is a meeting or a conference call, scheduled for anything from an hour or two to a day or two depending on the number of parties involved and the complexity of the matter at hand, between all the parties to a matter. This will include clients and lawyers, clearly, but may also involve other third parties such as banks (investment and commercial), accountants, consultants, tax advisors, even occasionally regulators. In a non-commercial setting it could involve civil and criminal authorities.

Ancillary documents (**'Ancils'**): These are documents which support major documents on a project. For example, when shares in a company are being sold, a share purchase agreement and a stock transfer form are probably sufficient to effect the legal arrangement. However, supporting those main documents will be others such as board minutes. These documents which, it must be emphasised, will vary from arrangement to arrangement, are prime territory for trainees.

Bible: Again, the preserve of trainees everywhere. A 'bible' is the commonly used term for the compilation of documents when a project is completed. Bibles once produced are sent to or shared with (if cloud-based) the clients, opposition lawyers, other advisors (financial, tax, other consultants). It's an admin job, but a satisfyingly final one.

Black letter law: The substance of law – cases, legislation, regulation

– and the ability to understand it and draft appropriately (e.g. 'a good black letter lawyer').

Bus Dev/BD (business development): Strictly, the process of generating work. However, often used much more broadly to indicate any relationship-building activities with clients (including in-house lawyers) and intermediaries (accountants, consultants, finance houses etc).

Capacity: A key question you will be asked time and again: 'Do you have capacity?' meaning 'Do you have time to do this work?' The question of capacity is filled with nuance. It will depend on the work you've already agreed to (even if it hasn't started), the views of your supervisor on taking work, whether you can delegate some of it (once that becomes appropriate) and so on. Whether or not you have capacity is something you will spend the rest of your career trying to figure out, at least until you can delegate at will, although even then the management of delegated work is a job in itself.

Certified copy: A copy of an original document where it is recorded on the face of the copy that it is a true copy of the original, signed by a solicitor usually in the name of the firm.

Client partner: As distinct from the matter partner (see below), the client partner will be responsible for managing the overall relationship with a client, providing a sense of consistency especially in a large commercial firm.

Comparison/redline/legal blackline: Given that the product of law firms is documentation of one sort or another, it will be no surprise that understanding what changes have been made to an edited document is critical. To do this, firms use comparison software (similar to the inbuilt capability in Word, but with additional features). The result is a document, normally in pdf or Word format, within which the differences – deletions and additions – from the older document are marked. If asked to run a 'comparison', a 'redline', a 'blackline', or any other term that implies a comparison, then this is what you need to do. 'Blackline' and 'redline' come from the way in which changes are identified, with red or black underlining.

Conflicts (conflict check): There are two sides to conflict checking. First, before a client is taken on by the firm (and, subsequently, before each matter for that client is accepted) a check is made to ensure there is no conflict of interest. A conflict of interest may take many forms, but at this stage would include things like acting against the would-be client or for another party on the same matter. The second stage of review is continuous: as the matter progresses, if a conflict of interest develops between either the client and the firm (including for these purposes individual solicitors in the firm) or between two clients. If it does, the individual (and usually the firm) must stop acting and other arrangements put in place. Although you're unlikely to be responsible for running conflict checks, you should pay attention to the way in which your firm carries them out and contribute all information you are asked for. The mechanism protects both the firm and its lawyers from accusations of impropriety (and, worse, possible negligence).

Continuing Professional Development (CPD): The term given to regular training to keep your professional skills up to date. The SRA regulates solicitors' CPD and takes an outcomes based approach, meaning that although there is a requirement to engage with CPD, the type and quantity of training that you do is not dictated: it must, however, be sufficient to address any gaps ('learning needs' in SRA parlance) you have identified in reflecting on your practice. For context, this is in distinction to a system, abandoned in 2016, which designated a set number of hours for CPD and resulted in people attending any old training session, whether related or not to their practice, in order to get the hours.

Corporate governance: The term given to the rules and procedures an organisation puts in place to direct and control its operations. It is driven by the provisions of company law, the regulatory environment within which that organisation operates, and in light of best practice suggestions provided by external bodies, such as the Chartered Governance Institute.

Data site/Data room: A secure, confidential, probably cloud-based document repository to which documents are uploaded by one set of lawyers (and their clients) for another (and their clients) to review. Often run by external providers, although occasionally larger firms have their own system. Similar to Dropbox, Sync and the like, but much more user-friendly, data sites can be reconfigured as clients and their advisors wish. You may also hear these referred to as data 'rooms', a throwback to the recent past where hard copy documents filled lever arch files and were stacked in dark rooms – it was a trainee's job to go and review the documents and report back. It sounds rather sad, but it was actually a good day out of the office unless you were stuck there for weeks. Today, you're only likely to come across a true data room if a document is deemed to be so sensitive that it can't be shared electronically. The moniker 'room' has stuck, however.

DMS: Stands for 'document management system' and is a generic term to refer to the document management software your firm will use. These systems are used to file and archive documents produced by all employees of the firm, giving a document a number, a version, a date of production and an author. Version control is very important, especially when multiple lawyers are working on the same document. Knowing whether a document is version 2 or version 10 allows you and your colleagues to monitor its life and move between sets of changes as needed.

Drafting: Used generically to refer to any sort of writing – you can 'draft' a document, an email, a chart, a timeline, a birthday card. This agrees with the standard use of the word – a preliminary copy of a piece of writing – but lawyers are particularly fond of the expression, perhaps because we write for a living.

Due diligence/DD: A phrase used to describe investigation and review. In the commercial/corporate world, investors or would-be purchasers will conduct due diligence of a business they wish to buy or invest in. Lawyers are often asked to conduct legal due diligence, verifying shareholdings, licences and so on, but the whole exercise can cover a much wider territory – finance, IT and regulatory matters (in the context of a heavily regulated industry like finance or healthcare).

Engagement letter (including terms of business): A very important document for law firms to provide to clients. It will describe the terms on which the firm is engaged, setting out the scope of the engagement, the agreed fee or method of establishing that fee, and any assumptions on which the terms have been agreed i.e. that the project will finish by a particular date. It will also include or incorporate by reference the firm's standard terms of business. The engagement letter has the dual purpose of ensuring the terms of the engagement are agreed before any substantial work is done (after all, there's nothing worse than doing work and realising that because terms weren't agreed then no-one's getting paid, or a very awkward conversation is needed) and fulfilling client care obligations imposed by the SRA.

Fee earner: Used to distinguish anyone who earns money from client fees from other staff.

File: Once a beautifully handwritten collection of letters, the 'file' is now almost certainly digital. A central repository will be available on your firm's internal systems (and through the DMS) where all emails sent, documents produced and file notes generated will be stored. All incoming communications relating to that matter should also be stored in that folder, including voice messages (which on most telephone systems now arrive as an email anyway). Everything should be recorded here. 'Opening the file' is the process by which the file is initially set up; each firm will do this differently, but it will involve identifying key actors on each side (including professional advisors) and a conflict check (see above).

File note: Best practice remains to make contemporaneous notes of meetings or phone calls unless the subject matter is trivial. Your firm will give you training on what records it expects you to make and retain, but as a general rule a call should be logged (start and end times), the attendees recorded, and a general note of the substance should be written up. For most calls, scanning written notes onto the system to be recorded on the file may be sufficient; for others, a formal memo may need to be written. Always, always, take notes. Getting into that habit just makes life easier and demonstrates your professionalism.

Freehand (or free drafting): Shorthand for making up the drafting rather than using an established precedent which would give you wording agreed and finalised in another project (or that is generally accepted). Some of the best and most frightening (professional) times are when you are called upon to free draft: at that point you are a lawyer with a pen, like many before you, and you have to make the words sensible and as watertight as you can.

Heads of terms (HoTs): A schedule setting out the key terms of a project or a deal. It is never agreed to be legally binding, but it has a moral force that is difficult to argue with as principals move forward with the transaction. It will summarise, for example, what is being sold, the price to be paid, arrangements for due diligence, the date by which final legal agreements should be in place and any other key terms the parties want to record upfront before entering into detailed negotiations.

House style: The presentation rules for documents issued by your firm. Standardising the work product for a firm is an important brand strategy and provides consistency across different departments.

HR/Human resources: Large law firms will have a separate department to manage HR issues; smaller firms are likely to outsource that responsibility or make it the responsibility of a general admin team (with outside support). Work out who your HR contact is because they are likely to be responsible for allocating seats and you may be able to express an interest in a particular field. It's also a useful contact to have for any employment related issues.

Mark up: The bread and butter for lawyers is negotiation with other lawyers. Any document you produce where another party is represented will need to be shared with those other lawyers and they are likely to have comments. They will send you back a mark up – a revised version of your document with changes they would like included (usually sent by way of a comparison document – see 'comparison'). You won't necessarily accept all the changes proposed (or any of them) – that's the nature of negotiation – but it will be the 'mark up' you discuss.

Matter: Another word for a project. A 'matter' could be an instruction to draft an appointment letter for a CEO, to represent a buyer of a business, or to act on a divorce.

Matter partner: The partner leading (or primarily responsible for) the matter, as opposed to the client partner who, as a reminder, is responsible for the client relationship. It may be the same person, it may not.

PA/Legal Secretary: PAs – formerly legal secretaries – are the backbone of any department. They tend to work for a number of people, perhaps a partner, a senior associate, a couple of associates/solicitors and a trainee. This means they are busy and need to make judgment calls about whose work takes priority. Don't be afraid to ask for help; they are the best source of advice in the firm.

Pipeline: Work that has yet to come in but is expected, or where instructions have been received but the project hasn't yet been allocated to a team. Shorthand for 'stuff that's going to hit your desk in the near future'.

PQE: Post-qualification experience – the number of years of experience under your belt from the date you qualified.

Precedent: A generic term for anything that can be used as a starting point for drafting. A previously produced agreement, a format for an article, a letter that can be amended and reused.

Red pen: A term used to describe revisions made by a senior i.e. 'Has she got out the red pen yet?' or 'Has it been red penned?' It happens to everyone; the point of the hierarchy in a law firm is that experience flows down and if you add to that different approaches to style it's not uncommon to have a senior completely rewrite your draft. It's reassuring and also sets you up for the times when work comes back with only minor changes (if any at all) – a satisfying day!

Redline: See 'comparison'.

Seat: A block of time you spend in a particular department over the period of your training, typically six months.

SQE: The Solicitors Qualifying Examination (1 and 2), the final assessment for all solicitors entering the profession. A large amount of material on the SQE, its introduction and implementation is available on the SRA's website.

SRA: The Solicitors Regulation Authority – the regulator for solicitors.

SRA Standards and Regulations: The key reference for professional obligations produced by the SRA, setting out '[t]he standards and requirements we expect our regulated community to achieve and observe, for the benefit of the clients they serve and in the public interest'.

TLAs: Three letter acronyms – try to avoid them or, if used, spell them out as frequently as style permits.

Traffic light system (or RAG coding): A system of using red, amber, green (RAG) to identify key issues. Used in many contexts, the standard implication is that a green label means 'just for information' or 'as expected', a red label means 'this is a problem' or 'this is an outlier which requires investigation', with an amber label identifying something in between. It's as simple as it sounds, once you know what it is, but regularly causes confusion. The difficulty is in making the initial evaluation leading to the allocation of a red, amber or green mark rather than any application of the system!

Utilisation: The main way of assessing how busy you are/have been, this is your time spent carrying out billable work against the total notional usual working hours available to do so (as a percentage). So, if your firm requires you to record eight hours of time per working day, after a working week the notional time recorded would be 40 hours. If you recorded 24 billable hours in that week, the rest made up of non-billable time, your utilisation would be 60% (24/40). If you recorded 60 billable hours, your utilisation would be 150% (60/40). It will be a running calculation throughout the financial year.

Vac (vacation) scheme: A short period of work experience at a firm, normally for two weeks.

Work in progress/WIP: This is used to describe the accrued time on a particular matter. So, if an employment matter has been running for some time with input from various parts of the firm, the WIP will be the total figure showing on the system for that matter i.e. the time recorded by each person multiplied by their charge out rate and aggregated. Many clients like to be kept appraised of the WIP levels and, even if they haven't asked, it is sensible to communicate those figures. Whether this is necessary will depend on the terms of the engagement letter, setting out the billing model – if a fixed fee has been agreed then it may be moot, but even then a senior might consider it appropriate to share how much WIP has been generated to make a commercial point. It's unlikely you will need to get involved in this kind of decision, but it's helpful to be aware of the term.

DOUBLE DUTCH: A GUIDE TO JARGON

With tongue firmly in cheek, these are phrases you will almost certainly come across and which, following an entirely unscientific review of colleagues and trainees, are deemed to cause the most confusion. Intended to give a general explanation of the terms; whether you use them or not is left up to you. Some are beautiful, some painful, all are commercial (rather than specifically legal) buzzwords at the time of writing.

80/20: Used as shorthand for 'make sure that your efforts are properly directed', this oft quoted but rarely understood phrase comes from management theory (the Pareto Principle) which is an observation that approximately 80% of output (e.g. sales) comes from 20% of input (e.g. customers). In other words, a small proportion of your overall effort will result in the majority of your results/successes. So consider carefully where you apply your energy. In law it tends to be used to mean that rather than trying to address every issue in a project, focus on those issues deemed to be material; the rest will fall into place.

Across this…: Mostly used as an interrogative ('Are you across this?'), this terrible saying simultaneously implies you should have a grip on all strands of a project (hence 'across') but that you probably don't. Translated as: 'Do you have any idea what's going on because you should?'

Close of play (close of business): The end of the working day. Contrary to first impressions, this is ambiguous: depending which lawyer you talk to, it can mean the standard end to the working day (say 5.30pm), the end of YOUR day, the end of your senior's day, midnight on the given day, or any time before morning. And all of this before you start dealing with different time zones! Check with the client what they expect; generally 'the end of the day' will have a context specific meaning.

Cold towel: Broadly to review (or delay) a decision so that it can be made calmly/not in the heat of negotiation. It's also often applied to the proof-reading of near final documents: 'I'll cold towel this and get back to you…'

Deep dive: An investigation into a particular issue or thing, resulting in (it is hoped) a detailed understanding.

(We won't…) Die in a ditch (over this): Usually used when pointing out a relatively minor point, agreeing that failure to accept a revised position won't mean pens down (see below), but emphasising it's something that probably needs to be sorted out at some point (possibly).

Drill down: To investigate further or to establish the full details.

Ducks in a row: A favourite with lawyers, you are likely to hear this on day one. Used to indicate the necessary level of organisation or a required (practically divine) alignment of all things necessary to accomplish the task at hand. 'We'll need a day or so to get our ducks in a row…'

Granular approach/level of granularity: Commonly used as a query: 'What level of granularity are you looking for?' i.e. do you want us to report on each of these things or will an overall summary do?

Helicopter back to that… (loop/circle back): A rather fun Americanism, used to imply a return to the issue under discussion at another time. Mostly used where the speaker has no idea of the answer to a question posed: 'Um, that's a good question, let's helicopter back to that…'

Home team: Those on the same side of a matter, lawyers, client and other professional advisors. Distinguished from 'the other side'.

Horse trading: To concede one point in return for a concession on another. Usually home team talk: 'We won't give this up yet; if we're not bothered about it, we can horse trade with it later'.

'I'll check my instincts, but…': Again, used where the speaker has no idea what the answer might be and is making something up on the spot. Essentially a caveat to what comes next: 'I'll need to check my instincts on this one, but I think I'm right in saying…'

Kick(ed) into the long grass: Postpone(d), often indefinitely.

Kick the tyres (look under the bonnet): You're probably familiar with this concept from (literally) buying a car. Often used in a commercial context to mean investigating a business or discussing a deal without committing to progressing. 'We're not looking to enter into heads of terms yet; we're just kicking the tyres and checking the figures.'

Low hanging fruit: Points of relatively small value or impact that can be negotiated quite easily; won't (or shouldn't) lead to protracted discussion and therefore can be dealt with swiftly.

Market: Shorthand for 'market standard', the position that is broadly acceptable or accepted as common practice throughout the relevant area.

P to P (principal to principal): Discussions between principals i.e. between clients rather than their respective lawyers. Often shorthand for a fundamental point which doesn't relate to or can't be resolved by agreeing wording between the lawyers and therefore requires a commercial discussion.

Parked: A point (or even an entire project) is paused to be resurrected at a later date (if at all). 'We'll park the variation deed for now, and concentrate on the objection letter'.

Pens down: To stop working on a project. Enjoyably evocative – imagine a fountain pen thrown down on the desk in despair.

Piece: A workstream or a discrete part of the project when discussed in a wider context. So, 'the employment piece [of the wider project] will need particular thought'. Ubiquitous.

Run it up the flagpole: Test out an idea, normally with the lawyers or principals on the other side. Similarly, 'try it for size'.

Something to hang our hat on: A starting point. Ok it might not be the final answer, but it's a promising beginning for discussion to move things on. Similarly, a useful factual starting point for negotiations.

Square the circle: To link things up – departments, people – to ensure that everyone on a project knows what everyone else is doing.

Take it offline: Take a discussion away from public negotiations/interactions and think about it privately. Often used in the context of all parties meetings where lawyers and clients can't communicate in freedom.

Touch base: Generally assumed to derive from baseball terminology; various online resources suggest that as a baseball player needs to touch each base as they run, it has become accepted as shorthand for briefly making contact. In legal and other professional contexts it's shorthand for 'get in contact with', whether via meeting, call, email or otherwise.

ACKNOWLEDGMENTS

This book came together over several years, with input directly or indirectly from lots of sources. There are, correspondingly, many people to thank.

The issues I've sought to address came from its subject: trainees. Those I've supervised over the last couple of decades, those from different teams and firms who spoke to me when doing the research for the book (extremely informally), and the pearls of wisdom proffered by former trainees as they took on a supervisory role themselves. I can't say thank you enough.

A shout out, too, to my own cohort of trainees. I learnt a tremendous amount from all of you.

Thanks to David, Helen and Hannah at Bath Publishing for their enthusiasm for the project, which was much needed when I despaired of finishing the book and sending it out into the world. Their input has been invaluable. Cheers, also, for tea.

Thanks to Beebs, Emily, Helen, Kelly, Lisa, Pardeep, Parm, Ryan, Sophie and Stas for reading an advanced draft. Your cheerful support was and is hugely appreciated; your collective eye for detail and narrative continuity second to none. Errors and omissions are my own.

Thanks to Andrew Masraf and David Stevenson for their appreciative comments, and to Andrew for taking the time to write the book's excellent Foreword. The vote of confidence from such respected practitioners and managers means a very great deal.

To the Overseer of the Affairs of the Palace: thanks for the comments and well done on supervising at least one trainee of the year (I'm sure there are other awards we don't know about). Thanks for supporting me always, giving up evenings and weekends so I could finish this.

And, finally, Thea and Zoë: another book to add to your library!

INDEX

A

Adding value	153
Advice to clients	84
All parties meeting/call	229
Ancillary documents ('Ancils')	229
Applying for jobs	24
Appraisals	116
Artificial intelligence (AI)	25, 112, 210
Asking questions	14
Associates	26, 27
managing associate	26
principal associate	26
senior associate	26, 27

B

Bibles	81, 230
Billing structures	33
Billing/time management	86
Black letter law	229
Building relationships	156
Bus Dev/BD (business development)	40, 85, 230

C

Capacity	230
Capped fee arrangement	36
Certified copy	230
Cheerful working	73, 149, 154
presentation	77
Client/matter numbers	102
Client partner	230
Clients	153
adding value	153
approach to	154
building relationships	156
cheerful working	154
emails and tone	158
following client instructions	157
Closing time	105
Collaboration	15
Comparison	230
Confidentiality	110
Conflicts	33, 34, 231
Continuing Professional Development (CPD)	55, 231
Corporate governance	231
Corporate Social Responsibility (CSR)	162
Counsel *See* Legal Director (LD)	
Covid-19 pandemic	9
Credibility	151

D

Data room	231
Data site	231
Dictation	109
Disbursements	35
Document management	83, 232
Doing the work	81
advice to clients	84
assisting with training	84
billing/time management	86
business development	85
document management	83
drafting engagement letters	84
helping out the partners	86
organising team socials	86
photocopying	81
preparing a bible	81
preparing a bundle	81
recruitment	85
research	84
taking notes and minutes and preparing file notes	85
Drafting	232
engagement letters	84
Dress code	42
Due diligence/DD	232

E

Effective time management	109
Engagement letter	35, 232
Environmental, Social and Governance (ESG)	163
Equity partners	29
Ethics	213
External training	52

F

Fee earners	233
File notes	233
Files	233
Firm life	161
Corporate Social Responsibility (CSR)	162
getting involved	161
law societies and local business organisations	167
leadership roles	167
newsletters	167
pro bono legal advice	164
Responsible Business	162
school support/school governors	166
social activities	162
special interest groups	166
sport	165
Fixed fee arrangement	35
Free drafting	233
Freehand	233
Further study	202

G

Generative artificial intelligence (AI)	112, 210

INDEX

Google notifications	15

H

Handovers	114
Heads of terms (HoTs)	234
House style	2, 234
Human Resources (HR)	234
Hybrid working	9, 214
mental health support	215

I

Internal training	51
'round table' sessions	51
Interview preparation	186
Invoicing	34
capped fee arrangement	36
fixed fee arrangement	35
time billed basis	35

J

Jobs list	24

K

Knowledge Lawyer
See Professional Support Lawyer (PSL)

L

Law as a business	32
Law societies and local business organisations	167
Leadership roles	167
Legal advice	33
Legal blackline	230
Legal Director (LD)	28
Legal Practice Course (LPC)	3, 8
Legal project managers	13

M

'Magic Circle' firms	35
Managing mistakes	89
being proactive	92
emails and other communication	90
first principles	90
how not to treat people	94
stress and coping	96
Managing time	101
capacity	105
closing time	105
communication	111
competing deadlines	110
dictation	109
effective time management	109
generative artificial intelligence	112
handovers	114
organising emails	112
time recording	101

Managing time *(cont)*
- to do list — 111
- triage — 111

Mark up — 234
Matter — 234
Matter partner — 235
Mental health support — 215

N

Newsletters — 167
Non-fee earning colleagues — 146
Note taking — 54

O

Office gossip — 148
Open plan working — 11
Organising team socials — 86

P

PA/Legal Secretary — 235
PAL System — 133
- application of — 138
  - acknowledge — 135
  - listen (or learn) — 137
  - prepare — 134

Paralegals — 26, 30
Partners (salaried/equity) — 29
Pipeline — 235
Post-qualification experience (PQE) — 235
Precedent — 235
Preparation — 7
Presentation — 3, 77
- cover emails — 79
- formatting — 79
- form of greeting — 79
- research — 77

Pro bono legal advice — 164
Professional Development Lawyer (PDL) *See* Professional Support Lawyer (PSL)
Professional indemnity insurance — 33
Professional requirements — 50
Professional Support Lawyer (PSL) — 28

Q

Qualification — 183
- interview preparation — 186
- process — 184
- staying in touch — 188

R

RAG coding — 236
Recruitment — 85
Redline — 230, 235
Red pen — 235
Reflection journals — 113
Remote working — 9, 15
Research — 84

INDEX

Resources, access to	15
Responsible Business	162
Role of the supervisor	130
Round table sessions	51
RSS aggregators	15

S

Salaried partners	29
School support/school governors	166
Seat 1: Commercial litigation	57
Seat 2: Planning	119
Seat 3: Corporate	171
Seat 4: Secondment	217
Seats	235
Secondment	191
further study	202
impact on job prospects	195
impact on personal life	195
practical considerations	194
reasons to consider it	192
self-development	195
types of	191
Self-directed learning	15
Social activities	162
Solicitors Qualifying Exam (SQE)	3, 8, 50, 207, 235
Solicitors Regulation Authority (SRA)	8, 235
SRA Standards and Regulations	236
training material	19

Special interest groups	166
Sporting or social events	40, 165
Standardised fonts	2
Stand up meetings	13
Staying in touch	188
Staying up-to-date	15
Stress and coping	96
Supervision	22, 129
'good' and 'bad' supervision	132
PAL System	133
personality	141
role of the supervisor	130

T

Takeaways	38, 47, 56, 87, 99, 118, 142, 152, 159, 169, 189, 204, 216
Taking notes and minutes of meetings/preparing file notes	85
Team culture	41
Terms of business	232
The first day	39
illustrative timetable	43
The future	207
ethics	213
generative AI	210
hybrid working	214
SQE	207
Three Letter Acronyms (TLAs)	236
Time recording	101

Traffic light system	236
Trainees	26, 30
Training	19, 49
external training	52
impact on career	55
internal training	51
'round table' sessions	51
professional requirements	50
responding to	53
note taking	54
Solicitors Qualifying Exam (SQE)	50
Training contracts	8
seats structure	20
Training courses	
structure	2

U

Utilisation	236

V

Vacation (vac) scheme	1, 236
Virtual meetings	12

W

Work experience *See* Vacation scheme	
Working from home	14
Work in progress/WIP	236
Work/life balance	12

Y

Your cohort and other support	143
credibility	151
non-fee earning colleagues	146
office gossip	148
personality	143